Chocolatherapy

Chocolatherapy

Satisfying the Deepest Cravings of Your Inner Chick

KAREN SCALF LINAMEN

Revell
Grand Rapids, Michigan

Published by Fleming H. Revell
a division of Baker Publishing Group
P.O. Box 6287, Grand Rapids, MI 49516-6287

Printed in the United States of America

Library of Congress Cataloging-in-Publication Data is on file at the Library of Congress, Washington, DC.

ISBN 10: 0-8007-3189-1
ISBN 978-0-8007-3189-2

For my sisters
Renee Berge and Michelle Willett.
If they ever make chocolate an illegal substance,
will you be my cell mates?

Contents

Appetizer   9

1. Hungry for a Change?   13
2. Visibility   21
3. Escape   33
4. Love   41
5. Perspective   52
6. Community   69
7. Context   80
8. Viscosity   93
9. Sleep   102
10. Clarity   111
11. Control   124
12. Transformation   137

The Chocolaphile Files   151

Appetizer

If you've ever done the emotional-eating thing, raise your hand. No, not the one holding the Twinkie. The other one.

The bad news is that stress and crisis can send us reeling toward the pantry. The even worse news is that stress and crisis are everyday ingredients in the mixing bowl of life. After all, if life ran smoothly most of the time, what would it matter if every few years we got stressed and happened to cope by eating too many desserts? (By the way, since *stressed* spelled backwards is *desserts*, shouldn't we treat *warts* with *straws*? Or drink *Evian* as an antidote to being *naïve*? Just wondering.)

No, the truly fattening truth is that—if your life is anything like mine—you get handed daily servings of stress and crisis, not to mention chaos, change, heartache, headache, and on special occasions, disillusionment à la mode. In fact, some days life feels like a more-than-you-can-carry smorgasbord, baby, second-helpings mandatory.

Chasing down all that stress with junk food—for medicinal purposes only, of course—is a tempting strategy. I don't know what your favorite binge-food happens to be (if it's celery, close this book immediately and give it to a normal friend), but when I'm on an emotional-eating bender, I reach for the chocolate. This is why my closet contains clothes ranging from size 12 to 24. But before you judge me as narrow-minded (albeit wide-hipped), let me assure you that I'm an equal-opportunity binger. This means I also reach for chips. And doughnuts. And—like last week's binge—Bit-O-Honey. You know what I'm talking about, right? Those chewy, bite-sized candies that taste like honey even as they extract all your fillings. Except I couldn't stop with just a bit. What I really ate was more like Bag-O-Honey. My dentist sent me a thank-you card. From a five-star resort in Fiji.

Because of my own experiences with emotional eating, I'm coming to a couple of realizations. The first is that dentists make way too much money.

The second realization has to do with my relationship with food. It's dawning on me that—when chaos, change, heartache, stress, or crisis send me foraging—I'm probably not *really* craving chocolate. At the risk of dissing my faithful cocoa friend, I'm realizing chocolate is often just a quick fix, a tasty substitute, a melt-in-my-mouth imposter. Indeed, whenever I'm careening toward ungodly amounts of comfort foods—chocolate or otherwise—chances are good that I'm longing for something else. Something healthier. Something deeper.

Which brings up an important question: What could our lives be like if, instead of trying to satiate those deeper longings with food, we stopped settling for quick fixes and tasty substitutes and gave our souls whatever they might *really* be seeking? Would we find greater contentment in our lives? Would we glean deeper understandings of ourselves and our emotions? Most importantly, would we finally be able to get into our skinny jeans *and stay there*?

What *are* we hungry for?

Maybe your closet isn't like mine. Maybe it doesn't contain dresses made out of ships' sails, but either way, you and I are still in the same boat. No doubt you know all too well the scenarios I'm describing. You're hungry too. Like me, sometimes you placate that hunger with instant s'mores you zap together in the microwave or bite-sized Snickers you lift from your kids' Halloween stash when they're not looking. (Note to self: Add graham crackers, marshmallows, and Hershey bars to grocery list.)

Not that those things are *always* bad.

Still, wouldn't it be great if we could feel a little less hungry? If we could feed our souls what they *really* need so that when we *do* decide to eat two quarts of Ben and Jerry's Chunky Monkey ice cream, we're doing it out of choice instead of compulsion? (Note to self: Add Chunky Monkey to grocery list.)

So that's what we're here to do. Figure out what we're really craving so we can start feeding our spirits the nutritious stuff we need to grow stronger seventeen ways. Or seventy. Or whatever.

People talk about cravings as if they're a bad thing. But I'm not so sure. I think cravings are cool. They're a sign of life. A symbol of potential. A portal to opportunity and change. If we satisfy those cravings with the right things, I think we can really grow as women and human beings. If we satisfy those cravings with the wrong things, we grow anyway, if you can call it growth when your swimsuit shrinks four sizes between summers.

And that's another benefit of figuring out what our hearts are really craving. By my calculations, if you and I could stop pigging out on comfort food for six months, we'd not only fit into sexy bikinis, we'd have lowered our grocery bills enough to afford extended vacations to some exotic location, like maybe the Fiji islands. And because we're going to look so hot, I think we should practice strutting a little between now and then. Just so we're prepared. Just in case we happen to run into anyone we know down there.

Wouldn't it be fun to see a dentist open wide and say, "Ahhhhh"?

1

Hungry for a Change?

I listened to my latest cell phone message and winced at the familiar voice. The poor woman deserved a medal. Maybe even cash prizes and gifts from our sponsor. Definitely a pat on the back.

"Hi Karen, Debbie again. Cheyenne and I came by earlier today with your cookies . . . I guess we missed you! We'll try again tomorrow."

I would have gladly called her back and told her when I'd be home, but she never left a phone number and each time she called, the word "unavailable" came up on my caller ID.

This tenacious woman had, to date, driven to my house on five different occasions trying to deliver the Girl Scout cookies I'd ordered from her daughter a month ago.

The good news is that she finally reached me by phone one Sunday afternoon. The bad news is that she woke me out of a dead sleep.

Groggy, I slurred, "Sure, anytime this afternoon's fine. When'll you be over?"

She said, "Actually, I'm calling from your driveway."

I felt bad answering the door with sleep wrinkles on my face and mascara smudges around my eyes, but after all I'd put her through already, I figured my beauty faux pas were the least of her concerns.

I invited her in, and we sat down at my kitchen table for the ceremonious writing of the check and cookie handoff. As she gathered her things to leave, I apologized for the game of hide-and-seek.

"No bother at all," she said lightly, waving my apology aside. "I'm glad it worked out. Last week the troop leader and I were selling cookies in front of the supermarket, and she asked if all my orders had been delivered. I told her they were all gone except for this one. She said we should combine your cookies with the ones we were selling at the supermarket, since sometimes people buy cookies out of obligation, not because they really want them. But I said no, you really wanted these cookies and I'd get them to you eventually. I told her, 'I could be wrong about this woman, but I don't think so.'"

I was touched. I'd only met this woman for five minutes last month when she showed up on my doorstep with her daughter. What a discerning person she was to realize I wasn't one of those deadbeat customers who ordered cookies merely

"When women are depressed, they eat or go shopping. Men invade another country. It's a whole different way of thinking."

Elayne Boosler

out of obligation and then abandoned their orders.

I said humbly, "Thank you for not giving up on me! But what made you so sure?"

She said, "One box? Maybe. But *nobody* feels obligated to buy fourteen boxes of cookies."

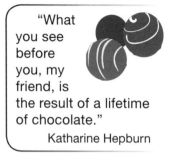

"What you see before you, my friend, is the result of a lifetime of chocolate."

Katharine Hepburn

Now that I think about it, maybe I *should* strive to be one of those deadbeats who orders cookies merely to feed her social conscience. I can only imagine what it would be like to invite a friend over for coffee, open a box of Girl Scout cookies, take one daintily, and reject the rest while saying nonchalantly, "I'm merely eating this cookie out of obligation. It's the least I can do for such a fine organization that has done so much for so many generations of deserving young women!"

It's a fun fantasy. Unfortunately, the truth is that I do *not* consume caramel-drizzled cookies out of obligation. I don't do chocolate for charity, and my addiction to pecan praline ice cream is not driven by philanthropy.

So why *do* I flock to junk food? And—more importantly—what's the first step toward change?

The Truth about Kit Kats and Corn Dogs

They say a journey of a thousand miles begins with one step. I say it starts with a trip to the bathroom. Or maybe a visit to the ATM. The other thing that can launch that kind of journey is an epiphany. I had that kind of moment recently. I was working on the outline for this book, sitting at my desk with a computer mouse in one hand and a box of Lucky Charms in the other, when it dawned on me that the first step toward change is a willingness to seek the truth.

Emotional eating and truth don't usually go hand in hand. In fact, denial often launches our binges as we eat to avoid pain or stress. And once we start eating, denial keeps us going strong. After all, when we're in the grip of a really good binge—the kind that can last anywhere from a couple of minutes to a couple of decades—do we *really* want to know how many calories or carbs we're consuming or even how much we weigh? I think not. This is why whenever I step on a doctor's scale, I close my eyes, stick my fingers in my ears, and hum "The Star-Spangled Banner." The *last* thing I want is to see the numbers or accidentally hear the nurse gasp as she records my weight.

But lately I've been trying something new. Lately, whenever chaos, change, or crisis threatens to send me on a junk food safari, I've tried hunting for the truth

A tasty sample from
The Chocolaphile Files

"For dessert, chocolate is truly the only choice—everything else, no matter how elaborate, is just a disappointing substitute.

Recently my husband brought home a five-pound bag of M&M's, thinking I would be thrilled at the sight of them. Instead I found myself filled with dread. . . . How is it that the thing you crave the most can simultaneously inflict such a deep fear of losing self-control and gaining weight?"

Diana Bender

instead. I've been doing this by asking myself three things:

1. Am I experiencing any discernable signs of real hunger? Stomach pains? Fatigue? Growls? Headache? Anything at all?
2. If not, then what am I feeling right now? Sadness? Loss? Stress? What is it? Can I put a name to my emotions?
3. If I close my eyes and imagine myself experiencing different emotions or circumstances, do I hit on anything that makes this craving suddenly feel a little less urgent?

I did this the other morning. I had just dropped my eleven-year-old daughter, Kacie, off at school when I found myself wrestling with a supersized craving for a McDonald's McGriddles breakfast sandwich. With no Golden Arches in sight, I was giving serious thought to driving several miles out of my way when I decided to do a little soul searching instead.

I asked myself, *Am I experiencing* any *discernable signs of real hunger?* The answer was no.

Okay, then what am *I feeling right now?* I didn't need to be a rocket scientist to figure that one out. I was feeling discouraged because I'd recently put on thirty pounds.

Finally I asked myself, *If I close my eyes and imagine myself experiencing different emotions or circumstances, what happens to my craving? Does it wax or wane?* I imagined a bunch of different scenarios. Suddenly I envisioned a scenario that made a difference. It was me, five pounds trimmer after a few weeks of healthy eating under my belt—or out from under my belt, as the case may be. Suddenly I felt a surge—both imagined and real—of hope. Wow! Who knew? Apparently the thing I was *really* craving was hope. Hope and maybe a little momentum. I realized these were the missing elements because, in the process of merely *thinking* about hope and momentum, I felt that McGriddles sandwich start to shrink from an overgrown obsession back into an ordinary breakfast food.

That was the really amazing part. It didn't seem to matter whether I actually *experienced* these new emotions and circumstances or simply *thought about* experiencing them. All I had to do was identify and envision the thing I was *really* craving and suddenly my splurge urge seemed tamable, kind of like when a half-ton Siberian tiger shrinks into a teacup kitten or—at the very least—a midsized Jaguar, air bags optional.

In the meantime, I've been checking with other women, asking them about the kinds of emotions and circumstances that do the same for them. And what I'm finding is that deep inside—somewhere beneath that uncontrollable urge to eat, shop, decorate, read romance novels, work out, scrapbook, spend time on-line, or anything else we embrace in excess—we're all pretty much craving the same stuff.

What *are* we craving?

Hope and momentum, definitely. We also crave community and perspective. Sometimes we long for trans-formation; at other times the thing we need the most is grace. We also desire answers and some sort of context in which to place those answers. Unconditional love is a biggie, as is clarity.

I'm even learning that sometimes what we're *really* craving are the resources and knowledge to manage the hormones in our own bodies. I've been doing some research on the biology of the binge, and turns out there are reasons why chaos, change, and crisis send us foraging. Yes, Virginia, there really *are* hormones at work in our bodies that make us crave junk food. Cravings are not necessarily about willpower. Sometimes they're the result of stuff going on in our bodies, meaning what we're really craving might be as basic as more serotonin or less cortisol in our systems, or even just a good night's sleep.

So these are the kinds of things we'll be exploring in the rest of this book. And by the time the final chapter brings us to the end of our little adventure, I have a feeling we'll each have made some valuable discoveries along the way.

Are you hungry for a change? If so, the next time you feel the urge to merge with all nineteen doughnuts left over from your son's science club meeting, reach for the truth instead. Ask yourself the questions I mentioned earlier to determine what you're *really* feeling.

Then pay attention to your answers.

In the meantime, let's take a look at a few of the *real* cravings that are in my life, in the lives of women I know, and most certainly in your life as well.

We'll start with our craving for visibility or, in other words, our longing to be known.

Living the Sweet Life

- What's wrong with downing a warm plate of mac-n-cheese when you're blue or a couple doughnuts when you're stressed? Is emotional eating *always* a bad idea, or can it serve a purpose? When do you think it crosses a line and can become a problem?

- Even if emotional eating isn't an issue for you, the topics in this book will still apply to you. Bottom line, this book is about the things you and I crave, things like unconditional love, a good dose of grace now and then, a healthy perspective on the things going on in our lives, clarity of thinking, and a sense of belonging to a vibrant community. Do any of these hit home for you? What can you add to the list? What are *you* hungry for?

- In the past, when something you craved didn't seem readily attainable—maybe you craved love but were single, or you longed for community but had just moved to a new city and didn't know a soul—how did you cope? Did you turn to food? Shopping? Alcohol? Prayer? Taking risks? However you coped, did it help you attain what you were *really* craving, or did it hinder your efforts?

2

Visibility

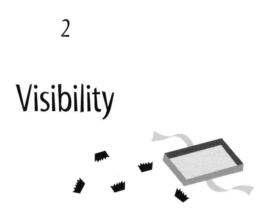

I remember the day I became visible again.

It was July about ten years ago, and I was attending the Christian Booksellers Association convention in Denver. While walking the half mile from my hotel to the convention center, I passed a man strolling the other direction. He nodded and said hello.

You could have knocked me over with a feather.

No, really. It probably doesn't seem like a big deal to you, but it really was a milestone for me.

You see, I'd been invisible for years, so the fact that this man actually saw *me* and not *through* me was a bit of a jolt. Of course, I'd been becoming gradually more visible for a number of months—I knew that—but it was still a very pleasant surprise.

My invisibility had always been a bit of a puzzle to me. I knew what had caused it—I'd gotten fat—but it still had the power to take me off guard. I mean, you would *think* that the larger someone gets, the easier she is to see. But I'd found just the opposite to be true: The bigger I became, the more I seemed to fade into the woodwork. Clerks, waiters, strangers on street corners seemed to feel more comfortable looking through me than at me.

So this particular hello really was a turning point for me. I'd recently lost sixty pounds, so I'd been looking forward to this moment, and when it finally arrived, I wasn't disappointed.

Of course, you and I both know that weight isn't the only thing that can render us invisible. Other things can make us feel unseeable and even untouchable. Some of these things include moving to a new city where we don't know a soul, feeling emotionally abandoned by a parent or lover, even getting divorced or never marrying and feeling relegated to some B-level social status as a result. A physical or mental disability can do the same thing. Even a mistake or tragedy—an unintended pregnancy, affair, bankruptcy, cancer, death—can leave us convinced that people around us are looking away in judgment or to avoid observing our pain. My point is, a lot of things can leave us feeling invisible. A lot of things can result in that now-you-see-her-now-you-don't experience.

And it's *never* a good feeling.

The truth is, being invisible hurts. I've wondered how something that's not there can still hurt, but maybe it's like that whole phantom limb thing. Someone loses an arm or leg, and for months or even years, their brain still registers sensation, like pain or even itching, where that limb used to be. Maybe being invisible is like that. After all, don't we all want to be noticed, to have people around us acknowledge our existence? It's pretty basic. And when it doesn't happen . . . ouch.

That invisible feeling feels *so* bad it's enough to drive me to the Little Debbies. I know other women who fear feeling invisible so much that they eat in *anticipation* of the pain, thereby setting themselves up for the very wound they long to avoid.

The longing to be seen is powerful. Primal, even. And no wonder! Being seen is foundational to being known. Invisibility, on the other hand, runs in the same crowd with isolation and even broken fellowship. I can't help but think of God strolling the fragrant paths of Eden calling, "Eve? Adam? Where are you?" A half-eaten apple lies in the shadows while Adam and Eve, hidden by foliage and fig leaves, remain unseen. Yesterday they were face-to-face with God. Now they are invisible, isolated, and in need of a Savior.

Here's Lookin' at Ya

Do you long to be known?

It's okay to say yes. After all, having our existence acknowledged is one of our most basic cravings. Maybe that's why babies come out of the womb wailing at the top of their lungs. It's definitely the reason Sandra Bullock's socially challenged character fell in love with a comatose patient and his boisterous family in *While You Were Sleeping.*

One time I fell madly in crush with someone because one of the first things he said to me was, "Tell me twenty-one things about you." His comment wasn't the magical part. The magic occurred over the next couple weeks as I came up with the twenty-one things he'd requested. My first dozen confessions were pretty shallow, the kinds of things any acquaintance might know. But as I dug deeper for things to reveal, I felt known in new ways, and my heart definitely got in on the act.

My friend Jen is one of five children. She describes her parents as kind and her childhood as relatively happy, and yet she doesn't feel close to either of her parents. When I asked why, she explained that with five kids, her parents stayed busy just making sure everyone was safe and fed and happy. Getting to know each child as an individual never seemed to be a priority. Even now Jen feels that neither her mom nor her dad has any clue who she really is. She considers herself a fairly well-adjusted person, but there's this little abandoned place inside that's hard to reach or salve.

Being "known" is one of the gifts we parents give our

A tasty sample from
The Chocolaphile Files

"Chocolate mellows me out. I train bank employees, and I tell the people in my classes they can bribe me with chocolate. Only one guy has tried it so far. He brought me some year-old stuff that looked pretty bad, so I told him he'd have to go stand in the corner."
Kelly Roberds

babies when we spend hours staring into their eyes and tracing the shape of their lips and memorizing the sound of their first laugh.

It's the dynamic at work when our husbands reveal something new or imperfect or private about themselves and it makes us fall even deeper in love with them (and all the while they're cringing because they're afraid their transparency will make us love them less!). In fact, one of the most romantic things any man has ever said to me began with the unlikely words, "I'm like a can of beans." He said, "I'm like a can of beans, and everyone else in my life is like one of those cheap aluminum can openers, the kind that always slip off the top of the can and the blades are always dull and the handles are too narrow and it's always a struggle. But you're like a Good Grips can opener, the kind with the thick rubber handles and the precision blade, and I find myself opening up to you in ways I've never opened up to anyone in my life."

Being "known" is intimacy at its best. Sometimes the Old Testament even uses the word *know* to describe the act of lovemaking. There's no way around it. Knowing is intimate. It's satisfying like nothing else. And it's how we're wired.

If one of our most basic cravings is the need to be seen and ultimately to be known, what's a girl to do?

If we're hungry for attention, I guess we could always try losing sixty pounds. We could also spike our hair and adopt multiple nose piercings. On a more satisfying level, we can make new friends and open up to old ones. If we're single, we can anticipate meeting soul mates who will desire to know us intimately. If we're married, we can set out with our husbands to explore uncharted terrain in search of deeper intimacy, navigating not by compass and beacon but by honing our skills at listening, vulnerability, transparency, and even risk.

We can even spend time getting to know ourselves. After all, feeling truly known by someone else can evade us until we take the time to really see and know ourselves. Remember Julia Roberts's character in *Runaway Bride?* After fleeing her fourth wedding, Maggie realizes she's been a chameleon, reinventing herself to meet the expectations of each fiancé without ever knowing who she is or what she wants out of marriage and life. After some serious soul searching, she eventually sets out to reclaim the heart of the last abandoned groom. Explaining to him why she had skipped out on so many weddings—including theirs—and why she subsequently had taken time away to find herself, she says, "When I was walking down the aisle, I was walking toward somebody who didn't have any idea who I really was. And it was only half the other person's fault, because I had done everything to convince him that I was exactly what he wanted. . . . But you, you knew the real me—I didn't. And you being the one at the end of the aisle didn't just fix that."

Feeling known by friends, parents, or husbands—and especially by ourselves—is a great idea. Actually it's more than just a great idea; it's vital to our emotional well-being and happiness. But I still have to wonder, are we missing something? Is there another place we can turn as well? Someone else whose attention can fill that void inside?

Can You See Me Now?

I have a story for you. It happened last summer. And if you ask me, it has something to say about this whole subject.

It all started when a close friend decided to give up smoking.

Again.

It had been an uphill battle. I won't kid you. For the umpteenth time, Linda had managed to stop smoking for a couple months before stress and cravings had their way and she picked up that next first cigarette. She was so upset with herself.

I hugged her and said, "Keep it up. One of these days you'll quit for good. Worst case scenario, even if you spend the rest of your life trying to quit and what *really* happens is that you spend two out of every four months without cigarettes, that's still an accomplishment. You'll still be so much healthier! So don't give up on quitting!"

About that time I attended a prayer meeting with my dad. Following dinner and worship, a man spoke for about half an hour about his relationship with the Lord. At the end he said, "If you need to talk to God about anything going on in your life, I'd love to pray with you tonight. I especially want to pray for anyone who is addicted to cigarettes and would like God's help in quitting."

As people gathered in small groups to pray, something stirred in my heart, and I walked to the front of the room. I said, "I'm here for a friend of mine who's tried to quit smoking for years. She can't do it on her own. She needs God to fight this battle for her. Can you pray for her?" Several people surrounded me in a tight little circle of love and prayers. We asked God to handle this problem from here on out. We acknowledged that only *his* efforts—and not Linda's or anyone else's—had the power to bring her the freedom she craved.

The next day I was driving to Linda's house with Chinese takeout when she called my cell phone and asked me to stop by the gas station and pick up a pack of cigarettes for her.

Whoa! What a mind-blowing request! In the eighteen years I'd known this woman, she'd never purchased a pack of cigarettes in my presence, much less asked me to buy one for her. She didn't even like to smoke in front of me, usually opting to smoke on the deck or in her car.

This was definitely a twist. And less than twelve hours after I'd approached God on her behalf! Linda waited for my answer. My mind raced. I knew I didn't have the power to save her from the habit she longed to break. Refusing her this one pack wouldn't make a dent in her addiction. But if I said yes, would I be hindering God in some way? I realized it all came down to this: did I believe in prayer or not? If the Holy Spirit was really going to win this battle for Linda, that meant *he* needed to intervene, not me.

I said, "Sure, what brand?"

Half an hour later, over lo mein and egg rolls, I debated whether to tell her about last night's prayer. In the end I was silent for the same reason I'd gone ahead and bought her that pack of Virginia Slims. Was God really God or not? Did I believe he could fight this battle for Linda and win? If so, I needed to shut up and watch. Besides, if I told her about the prayer, she'd probably feel pressure to try to quit again in her own power, and we already knew how well *that* worked! No, this was God's deal.

I never said a word.

Two weeks later we were hiking near my house when she suddenly announced, "Hey, guess what? I'm quitting smoking again."

My ears perked up. "Really?"

"I know it's the same ol' song and dance, but I haven't had a cigarette in a week and something feels different this time."

"Like what?"

"It's never been this easy. Never. Like it's not even a struggle. In fact, you know what I think?"

"Hmmmm?"

"I think God's helping me this time. I can't think of another explanation. Any other time I've quit, by now I'm going nuts. This time I hardly have any cravings at all!"

I still didn't say a word. Was God answering my prayer? Time would tell.

Three and a half months later, Linda was still smoke-free. Best yet, she was ecstatic over how easy it had been. We were sitting at a patio table on my back deck when I knew the moment had arrived.

I said, "I have a secret to tell you."

"Ooh, I love secrets! Who's it about?"

"You."

"Even better!"

I said, "Remember four months ago when I went to that prayer meeting with my dad? That night they prayed for people who wanted to quit smoking, and I went forward and asked them to pray over me *for you*. We asked God to fight this battle for you, to do it through *his* efforts and not yours. One week later you stopped smoking, and you haven't looked back since. I didn't tell you sooner because I didn't want either one of us to wonder, was it Linda or was it God? We don't ever have to wonder. God did this for you."

Linda was bawling by then. Come to think of it, so was I.

A box of Kleenex later, we were marveling at the whole thing when Linda said, "I'm glad the cigarettes are gone. I'm thrilled. That's a huge deal for me. But Karen, do you know what this *really* means to me? It means he's aware of me. He showed me he knows that I exist, that he cares about *me*. Even when you know God is there, sometimes you wonder if he's really aware of what's going on in your life. But now I know. He paid attention to *me*. He did this for *me*."

She looked toward the mountains and smiled. "He sees me."

Someone to Watch Over Me

Our desire to be known intimately by a personal and loving God isn't exactly a modern-day invention. In fact, it's as old as the hills.

An ancient text that always hits home for me is Psalm 139. Reading these words, there's no escaping David's deep longing to be known—and his awe when he discovers that the One who knows him more intimately than anyone else is none other than God himself. As you read his words, do what I do and embrace them as your very own:

> You have looked deep into my heart, LORD, and you know all about me. You know when I am resting or when I am working, and from heaven you discover my thoughts. You notice everything I do and everywhere I go. Before I even speak a word, you know what I will say, and with your powerful arm you protect me from every side. I can't understand all of this! Such wonderful knowledge is far above me. . . . You are the one who put me together inside my mother's body, and I praise you because of the wonderful way you created me. Everything you do is marvelous! Of this I have no doubt. Nothing about me is hidden from you! I was secretly woven together deep in the earth below, but with your own eyes you saw my body being formed. Even before I was born, you had written in your book everything I would do. Your thoughts are far beyond my understanding, much more than I could ever imagine. I try to count your thoughts, but they outnumber the grains of sand on the beach. And when I awake, I will find you nearby.
>
> Psalm 139:1–6, 13–18

The next time you and I feel invisible, sure, we could reach for the chocolate or—in a moment of attention-seeking resolve—the romaine lettuce and fat-free dressing. Or we could spend an hour with the God who sees us fat or thin, awake or asleep, outspoken or silent, even born or unborn!

Our craving is real. It demands satisfaction. Better than chocolate, better even than a Good Grips can opener, there is a God who sees—*really* sees—you and me.

Living the Sweet Life

- If a new acquaintance asked you to share twenty-one things about yourself, what would you choose to reveal? Go ahead. Make a list. It's fun. You might be surprised at what makes the list and what doesn't.

- As you read Psalm 139, did anything strike home? What was your favorite phrase or thought? Why was it meaningful to you?

- Name three positive things you can do the next time you feel lonely or invisible that don't involve calories. (Yes, if you're married, you can say *sex*. In fact, I'll be disappointed if you don't!)

- If someone were to ask you if God sees you, how would *you* answer?

3

Escape

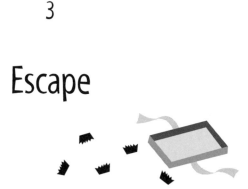

Do you ever find yourself mixing weird cocktails of unrelated activities?

One time I was on the phone with my editor, and she heard noises in the background and asked me what else I was doing. I had to admit that in addition to discussing the outline of my next book with her via the phone tucked between my ear and shoulder, I was rinsing spaghetti in the kitchen sink while nursing my ten-month-old by balancing her on one hip with my blouse hiked up to my neck.

It's just weird.

People have come up with a very respectable name for this kind of bizarre behavior. Now we can excuse nearly any combination of activities by saying haughtily, "Pardon me, I'm multitasking."

Talking on the phone to your boss while checking email and instant messaging your sister in Seattle? Multitasking.

Driving on the highway while brushing on mascara and dialing your dentist on your cell phone to schedule your next teeth cleaning? Multitasking.

Balancing your checkbook while making love to your husband? You got it: multitasking.

The fantasy is that multitasking saves time and energy and makes our lives run more efficiently. The reality is that it merely makes our lives more jam-packed and stressful than before. It's one more example of the curse of twenty-first-century living as we fall deeper into the trap of juggling too many things at once.

The Great Escape

Not long ago I found myself in the grip of that "Life is too crazy, somebody get me outta here!" feeling. Looking back, I probably should have logged onto eBay, bought a case of Calgon bath powder, and locked myself in the bathroom until spring.

I ate an entire box of Girl Scout cookies instead. And I'm not talking about those anemic Thin Mints, either. I'm talking about those amazing Samoas all drenched in caramel, layered with toasted coconut, and laced with chocolate stripes.

Granted, if you are a card-carrying Girl Scout cook-ieholic, you're not overly impressed with my confession

Pampering that's calorie-free *and* chocolate? Pinch me, girls, I'm dreaming!

Bathing in Chocolate

Philosophy's Chocolate Ice Cream three-in-one shampoo, body wash, and bubble bath is one hundred percent calorie free. You scream, I scream, we all scream for this 16-ounce chocolate-scented treat. Sold online at Philosophy.com and at Nordstrom, Macy's, and other fine department stores.

Does Chocolate Light Your Fire?

Mint chocolate chip ice cream candles made of vegetable wax that burns cleanly and evenly—sounds good enough to eat! Available in 22-ounce size at select White Barn Candle Co. and flagship Bath & Body Works stores, or visit BathandBodyWorks.com or call 1-800-756-5005.

Caffeinate Your Skin

Stimulate, exfoliate, and hydrate with Sephora's Full-Caff Non-Fat Double-Whipped Body Blend Set. Set includes a 7-ounce Coffee & Cream Morning Body Scrub, 1.7-ounce Cappuccino Creamer Whipped Body Delight, and a calorie-free loofah. Visit Sephora.com to order or locate stores, or call 1-877-SEPHORA.

Redefine "Chocolate Kiss"

The next time your lips crave chocolate, smooth on a Cocoa Butter Lip Care Stick. Visit TheBodyShop.com to order or locate stores, or call 1-800-BODYSHOP.

Pamper Your Piggies with Chocolate

Create your own chocolate paradise with Bella Lucce Dutch Chocolate Decadence Moisturizing Syrup. Infused with French cocoa and organic honey for silky soft pampering of your feet or whole body. Visit ChocolateLotus.com or call 1-813-956-3449.

because you happen to know there are only fourteen of those babies in a box. But before you discredit my pain and label me a lightweight, let me assure you that the box of Girl Scout cookies was only a precursor to the rest of the evening, during which I went on to consume four slices of buttered sourdough toast, a bag of Twix minis, and the last piece of two-week-old chocolate birthday cake. The cake was a little dry. Thank goodness the ice cream moistened it up.

As all those sugary carbs began making their way into my bloodstream, I started to feel calmer. A lot calmer. In fact, the word *la-la-land* comes to mind—which makes a lot of sense considering that those carbs were providing my brain the glucose and tryptophan it needs to create serotonin, the anti-stress, feel-good hormone that acts like a mild sedative as well.

And as for all that sugar? The truth is that it shot straight into my bloodstream, causing my blood sugar levels to first spike, then plummet, making me feel sleepy and impairing my concentration and memory. It probably numbed me out in other ways as well since sugar is thought to help block pain. Pediatricians say newborns aren't nearly as upset about getting a shot or having blood drawn after they've been given a sugar-coated pacifier.

No wonder you and I turn to junk food to help us zone out when our lives feel stressed or broken! In very measurable ways, junk food offers us disconnection and relief. We chocoholics moan over our chocolate as if we're enjoying a little bit of heaven, but if you ask me, our cocoa obsession is more accurately described

Out-of-This-World Chocolate

In 1981 the first space shuttle astronauts chose M&M's as part of their food provisions.

by a term borrowed from Eastern mystics. Chocolate, it would seem, is not unlike a ticket to Nirvana. And you can forget Ticketmaster—I'm not talking Nirvana *grunge* but Nirvana *zen*.

Buddhists define Nirvana as a mental state of disinterested wisdom. Hindus say it's the extinction of attachment. The dictionary describes it as oblivion to care or pain. In other words, Nirvana refers to a pleasant state of disconnect. What a perfect description of what happens when we use food to hush the din of chaos or pain in our lives!

But here's the rub: The morning after my Girl Scout cookie binge, I got on the scale. If chocolate had indeed transported me to Nirvana, it must have been a round trip, because at some point during the night I'd not only been dumped back home, I'd been dumped home fatter than when I left.

I *hate* when that happens.

Loading Zone Only

Apparently zoning out on junk food has its drawbacks. Who knew?

Nevertheless, the need to disconnect now and then is a valid one. I think there are times in every woman's life when a little disinterested wisdom, detachment, and oblivion are just what the doctor ordered.

But even when we have a legitimate need to get up and get away, does it *have* to be to McDonalds? And when we long for life to give us a break, can't we settle for something besides a piece of that Kit Kat bar?

Look, I hate saying this since there are still nine boxes of Girl Scout cookies waiting for me in the pantry, but I'm going to take a deep breath and blurt it out anyway: The next time I'm stressed, I promise I'll at least consider a few calorie-free distractions instead of lunging immediately for the carbs like I usually do. Would you think about doing the same?

What kinds of things might work for us? Pretty much anything that sends us to a happier place. It might be a long talk or a brisk walk. A computer game. A pedicure. Even praise and worship. I've noticed that when I'm busy thinking about myself, praise and worship can feel like little more than a sing-a-long. But when I force my thoughts away from myself and let my imagination dwell on the One I'm singing to, it's a different experience altogether.

How else can we escape?

I have one friend who enjoys zoning out on a tread-

"Researchers have discovered that chocolate produces some of the same reactions in the brain as marijuana. The researchers also discovered other similarities between the two, but can't remember what they are."

Matt Lauer
on NBC's *Today*

mill. Even I—the girl who flunked PE in high school and thinks "weight training" has something to do with using a girdle to keep your stomach in line—have to admit that exercise is a great way to escape stress and even emotional pain. My friend Eilene has a different method of escape. Last summer she shooed her husband and teenagers out the door on a camping trip. With the house all to herself, she spent the next four days eating nothing but cottage cheese while reading books and lounging in her favorite easy chair. Naked.

And, of course, now that I've gone and mentioned naked, we might as well talk about sex.

Recently, while in the middle of a particularly stressful couple of months, I found myself desperate for something, anything, that might distract me for even a little while. I craved something more riveting than a movie. More intense than dark chocolate. In essence, I longed for something to consume me whole, transporting me completely and utterly into another world, if only for a little while. I racked my brain. I'd had that feeling before. But what had caused it? Think, girl, think . . .

Oh. Well. Of *course*.

Are you married? Are you married and stressed? Maybe your marriage *makes* you stressed. It doesn't matter. Unlike your unmarried girlfriends who make do with movies and chocolate, you, my friend, are within arm's reach of one of the most effective methods of escape known to humankind. Yes, I know he snores. Get over it. And I realize your marriage isn't perfect, but why throw the baby out with the bath water? And while you're at it, consider checking your baggage at the bedroom door:

Making passionate love to your husband tonight doesn't *have* to mean you forgive him for forgetting your anniversary last month, although you'll be happier if it does.

Escape is good. Creative escape is even better. Non-fattening, rejuvenating escape is the very best. And when it comes to multitasking, maybe there's good news after all. The next time I get the urge to do several things at once, I think I'll try Eilene's eating/reading/naked-lounging thing.

Some weird cocktails of unrelated activities are simply meant to be.

Living the Sweet Life

- What kinds of stresses or events make you crave escape?
- Describe two of your favorite escapes: one that puts on the pounds and one that's calorie-free.
- What do you think about the relationship between escape and faith? Is escape a God-idea, considering he told us to take a day of the week and set it aside for rest and rejuvenation, or does our desire to escape mean we're doubting God's ability to take care of us?

4

Love

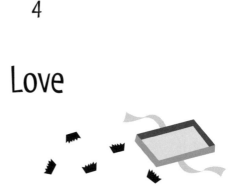

One Saturday morning about five years ago, Kaitlyn and I found ourselves in the kitchen microwaving s'mores.

Yes, yes. I know s'mores are *supposed* to be a campfire treat, but do you realize how long you have to wait to eat a campfire s'more? Sometimes, in the grip of an aggressive craving, a girl simply can't take the time to lug logs, find matches, crumple paper, make fire, coddle coals, and roast marshmallows. Sometimes she's gotta act fast.

Any serious chocoholic knows this. Which is why on this particular day, as Kaitlyn deftly prepared to microwave an entire plate laden with graham crackers, chocolate chips, and marshmallows for our pig-out pleasure, I watched her proudly and thought, "My baby's growing up."

And indeed she was. She had just turned fifteen. To celebrate, her dad and I bought her a silver Claddagh ring. I'm sure you've seen the design: two hands holding a crowned heart. We'd given her the ring along with a letter in which I explained our thoughts behind the gift. Here's how that letter began:

> Kaitlyn, your dad and I wanted to give you something to remind you, every day, of who you are in Christ. That's why we picked this ring. I know some of your friends have rings like it from their folks, and it means various things, but here is what it means to us: that you are a princess, that you are greatly loved by your heavenly Father, and that he holds your heart securely in his hands now and for eternity.

The microwave dinged. I hollered out the front door at Kacie, who was at that time all of six. Leaving her post in the flower bed where she had been collecting treasures, my little tomboy joined us for s'mores at the kitchen table. Watching my two princesses—one on the brink of womanhood and the other with dirt under her nails and pebbles in her pockets—my heart gave a bittersweet little wrench. They had so much to look forward to—so many joys to embrace and mistakes to make and gems of wisdom to acquire and losses to grieve. Watching my girls enjoy their s'mores, I thought about the rest of the letter I had written to Kaitlyn:

Act like a princess, sweetheart. Let this ring remind you every day to let your words and thoughts and deeds be those befitting of royalty.

Yet even as I write those words, I know you will make mistakes—small ones and big ones too. When that happens, run home fast, back to the "palace," back to your Father's arms, because here's the amazing truth: even when you forget to *act* like a princess, you still *are* one. Princesses don't get to be princesses because they *act* a certain way; they get to be princesses because they were *born* that way. They're not princesses because they never mess up but because of their relationship to the King. Royalty isn't based on behavior; it's based on blood.

Did Kaitlyn have any idea what those words meant? I hoped so! When it came to the idea of unconditional love, I desperately wanted both of my daughters to understand at an early age what it had taken me nearly forty years to figure out for myself.

When She Was Good, She Was Very, Very Good . . .

My story had gone like this: Growing up, I'd always felt loved by my parents, but then again, I'd also been a pretty obedient kid who tried to play by the rules. That meant I'd never really tested the whole "unconditional love" thing.

Suddenly, in my late thirties, I found myself in the midst of a really tough time. My marriage was a mess. I was clinically depressed. I also felt angry, rebellious, and disillusioned with everything I'd been brought up to believe, including my faith in God. (Note to my most faithful readers: this personal crisis in my life occurred after I wrote *Just Hand Over the Chocolate and No One Will Get Hurt* and before I wrote *Sometimes I Wake Up Grumpy and Sometimes I Let Him Sleep*. When you read *Grumpy*, you'll see that it addresses a lot of these kinds of issues, including depression, emotional pain, and loss of faith.)

How did my parents respond to me during this time? They hurt with me when I hurt, encouraged me when I messed up, and loved me always. My relationship with them felt more humble and transparent and intimate than it ever had before. It dawned on me that even though I'd never plumbed the depth of their love with my failures before, they had *always* loved me this much! So *this* is what unconditional love felt like! Wow! Who knew?

These memories and others meandered through my mind as I enjoyed the last of the s'mores with Kaitlyn and Kacie. I longed for my daughters to understand and experience unconditional love, just as I had. I wished they could learn this lesson the easy way, by just listening to their mom! Unfortunately, they would probably end up understanding it best

> ### A tasty sample from
> # The Chocolaphile Files
>
> "Recently I was overwhelmed with work and totally stressed. I went to the store to get cat food and they had Hamburger Helper on sale, and just the idea of it made me feel better. We used to eat this a lot growing up. . . . There are certain things that to me symbolize good experiences from the past, like Dad making hamburgers from freshly ground beef and the taste of homemade malts."
>
> Laura Lisle

as they experienced their own failures and crises, just as I had.

A few months later, my publisher asked me to write a children's book. I liked the idea but had no clue what I might write about! Then one afternoon while watching Kacie stuff her pockets with something new—this time it was pillbugs—I found myself asking the question, "What if there was a tomboy princess who couldn't seem to act like a princess no matter how hard she tried?" And Princess Madison was born.

"All I really need is love, but a little chocolate now and then doesn't hurt!"
Lucy Van Pelt in the comic *Peanuts* by Charles M. Schulz

How cool was *this* going to be? Through the adventures of a fictional six-year-old tomboy princess, I'd get a chance to write about all the neat truths my recent struggles had taught me about unconditional love. I was so excited!

I thanked God I'd learned my lesson. My experience with my folks had given me a much better understanding of my relationship with my heavenly Father. Still, I couldn't have been happier that my lessons on this subject were over. Case closed. End of story. The end.

Little did I know they had barely begun.

Grown-up Princesses Need Love Too

Six months later, my husband and I separated and began the heart-wrenching process of divorce. No one seemed surprised. We had struggled for twenty-one years. One time I told a friend that our marriage was like a glass vase that had shattered into a thousand slivers and shards. Larry and I had been trying to glue the shards of glass back together for a very long time, but it didn't seem humanly possible, and all we ever managed to do was cut ourselves more deeply on the broken pieces. We both knew God could put the vase back together and kept trying to hang on as long as possible. But it had already been years, and I was so *very* tired of cutting myself daily on the slivers of glass. I knew that without a miracle, one day I would take a broom and sweep the broken pieces away.

When that day came, I felt like such a failure I could barely breathe. And if breathing felt difficult, praying felt positively impossible. I stopped talking to God altogether. It wasn't out of rebellion but out of brokenness. All my failures up until now had felt the size of river rock. This was Mount Rushmore. How could I even *think* of approaching a holy God now?

One day my mom got my attention by saying, "Regardless of what happens to your marriage, *don't leave your relationship with the Lord!*" I thought about her words for weeks. Even if I could believe that God still wanted a relationship with me, how could I ever approach him? What words could I possibly say?

One afternoon I was cleaning a little rental house that Larry and I still owned, getting it ready for new tenants, when something broke inside of me and I found myself collapsed with grief in the stairwell, weeping wildly. I had wondered what I might say, but now the words flowed like water out of my broken heart.

"God, we failed miserably at this thing called marriage. We failed each other, we failed our girls, and we failed you. How can I even be in your presence? How can I dare call you Father? I can't even begin to live up to what I think a 'good Christian' should be. And yet . . . I miss you. I need you. But flawed as I am, I have no idea how to even start to be in a relationship with you. Please show me how to begin."

You know, it's easy to say "I love God and he loves me" when, in the world's eyes, you're doing everything right and living up to "the standard." But when you're floundering in a mess of wounds and mistakes—whether you created them yourself or you've been subjected to the decisions of someone else—it's a lot harder to feel like you belong in any kind of relationship with a perfect Father.

For most of my life I had approached God, yes, as my kingly Father but also with a bit of the smug confidence of the kind of daughter who has learned to play by the rules and feels pretty proud of herself as a result. Suddenly I'd turned into another kind of daughter, a very humbled princess with a muddy frock, crooked crown, skinned knees, and broken heart. What kind of relationship could we possibly have now?

Daddy

I really wrestled with that question. Then one day I asked myself, "Okay, think about your earthly dad.

How have you related to *him* through all this? And what would happen if you started to relate to your heavenly Father in the same way?"

The truth was, I'd needed my dad through this. I'd needed his strength. His wisdom. And my mom's as well. They hadn't been able to spare me from what I was going through, but they hadn't rejected me either.

My relationship with God took on a whole new dimension at that point. I'd always called him "Father," but suddenly that felt too formal. I began to call him "Babba," which means "Daddy" in Chinese.

Recently I found myself at Home Depot buying, I don't know, lightbulbs or something. Striking up a conversation with a cashier in her late fifties, I asked if she had family in the area. She said, "Both my parents died about five years ago. I'm an orphan."

An orphan. The phrase conjures up images of someone small, someone lost, someone abandoned too fully too soon. Someone longing for a porch light at dusk. At first those images seemed incongruent with the woman before me with nearly six decades on this earth. But as I thought about it I realized that, no matter how old we are, we never outgrow the longing for home.

I'm lucky. I have wise and loving earthly parents who have modeled for me the kind of relationship I can have with my heavenly Father.

I realize a lot of people aren't so lucky. As dads go, there's a huge range out there. There are absent dads and angry dads. Clueless dads and wise dads too. Some dads see the glass as half full. Some see it as half empty and figure if they're going to fill that empty space with something, it might as well be beer. Some dads carry the weight of the world on their shoulders. Others carry the weight of the world on one shoulder but try to leave the other free in case their kids need a place to cry or a spot from which to try to touch the moon.

While dads aren't exactly universal in nature, what is universal is our longing for a really great one. I don't know what kind of dad you had. My most heartfelt hope is that he was really amazing, just like mine. But either way, you and I are created to long for the same thing.

If I could describe that longing with an image, it would be this: a father cupping the face of his daughter in his hands, looking deep into her eyes and saying, "Hey, you're mine. You belong to me. Whether you're clumsy or poised, grumpy or kind, good or bad, serene or mad . . . whether you behave like the perfect princess or you mess up royally . . . none of that changes the fact that you belong to me and I love you."

Best of all, God is exactly that kind of father, and he longs to be that kind of father to you. How does that happen? Think about how you got into your earthly family. Trust me, your behavior wasn't a factor. How "good" you were as a fetus had nothing to do with it. Instead, you became a part of your earthly family through bloodline or adoption. Likewise, the blood of Jesus makes it possible for you to be adopted into God's family. In fact, adoption through Jesus is the *only* way into this family. And since your place in this family wasn't earned with perfect behavior, you can't unearn it when you mess up.

I don't fool myself anymore by thinking my own lessons on this subject are over. Of course, I'd be thrilled if I never stumbled or failed again, but with or without skinned knees I'm learning how to appreciate the kind of transparent, intimate relationship God longs to have with his children.

I eventually wrote my children's book. Three of them, in fact. In each book my six-year-old tomboy princess learns something new about the depth of her father's love for her. My daughters love the stories—and why wouldn't they? Princess Madison was inspired by both of them! But of course the message is for all of us. Maybe it can be a reminder that no matter how old we get or how unworthy we might feel, we're loved by a God who longs for us to call him Daddy.

Living the Sweet Life

Dear Jesus,

I'm hungry for a relationship with a loving heavenly Father. I long to be a princess, to belong to the King of Kings. The bad news is that I've got skinned knees and a muddy frock and I could never in a million years earn my way into your family with my behavior, no matter how hard I try! The good news is that because you died on a cross and took upon yourself the punishment that should have been mine, I don't have to. Please accept me into your family just as I am, fill me with your Holy Spirit, and help me begin, this very minute, a life-changing relationship with you. Amen.

Because Real Women Don't Need Cookbooks

Microwave S'mores

Place a graham cracker square on a plate or paper towel. Sprinkle chocolate chips on the graham cracker. Place one large marshmallow on top of the chips.

Microwave until the marshmallow swells up HUGE. Take out of the microwave and smoosh with a second graham cracker square. For chewier s'mores, microwave a little longer.

If you want any of these for yourself, you'd better make a lot and keep our mom out of your kitchen.

Kacie and Kaitlyn Linamen

5

Perspective

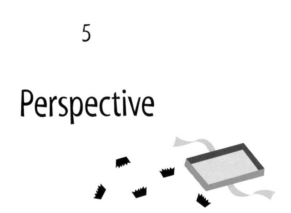

Four years ago, summer was drawing to a close and my yard was sporting the kind of untamed look that causes neighbors to sell their homes and purchase condos.

It even made *me* want to move away, and it was my yard.

Of all the houses I'd lived in before this one, no yard had ever been this out of control. When I was growing up, my dad had hired neighbor boys to keep our lawn short and orderly. When I was married, my husband mowed our lawn himself on weekends.

Even this lawn had been well cared for when my daughters and I had moved here ten months earlier. But somehow in the time I'd been in charge, something insidious had been happening. Grass had begun behaving badly, growing wildly in some places, refusing to budge in others, and insisting on turning brown in rebellious patches. Morning glories had overtaken the rosebushes, cocooning them in tiny, viney strands that were beautiful in a claustrophobic kudzu kind of way. The aspen tree in front of the picture window had apparently morphed into some kind of egotistical mad scientist, having cloned itself into literally dozens of three-foot-high saplings called—of all unpleasant things—root suckers.

As scary as my lawn had become, something about all the wildness felt familiar. This was so perplexing to me that I found myself mulling it over one morning while sitting on my front porch steps, a cup of coffee in my hands. I kept trying to figure out why I felt so much at home in such a disorderly yard, a yard unlike any I'd been associated with in my life.

After a while I gave up trying to figure it out. Besides, Kaitlyn—who was sixteen by then—was dressed and ready to go to the mall for a long-awaited shopping trip.

Kaitlyn and I had a total girl morning. We drank coffee. We window-shopped for lingerie. We got free department store makeovers which apparently transformed us into creatures infinite not only in beauty but also in credit, because I proceeded to charge several hundred dollars in cosmetics and did it euphorically to boot, and then I topped off the day by buying several new dresses for Kaitlyn. As we left the mall, my daughter absolutely glowed—I thought probably from all the lavish attention, but she might simply have worked up a sweat carrying all those shopping bags. Either way, she seemed thrilled and had the wisdom and good grace not to remind me that I'd been promising her this makeover ever since she'd turned thirteen.

Of course, if she *had* complained, I might have been tempted to tell her to take a number and get in line. In the ten months I'd been a single mom, it seemed I'd fallen behind in every area of my life. There were dishes in my sink that had been there since the Reagan administration. My publisher wanted Robert Stack to feature my unmet deadlines on an upcoming episode of *Unsolved Mysteries*. I couldn't have moved the bills and paperwork off my mahogany dining room table even if I'd wanted to—the piles had been there so long the sun had bleached the wood around them to a lovely shade of pecan. With so much on my mind, I'd forgotten to retrieve Kacie from school so often she'd resorted to setting an alarm clock to go off every afternoon to remind me to pick her up. Worst of all, I was *way* overdue for a salon appointment and my roots were showing. In light of all this, the fact that I'd been promising Kaitlyn this shopping trip for several years seemed like a rather small hiccup.

As if I needed yet another reminder, as we returned to the house and pulled into the driveway, *right* there, just where I'd left it three hours earlier, sat Exhibit Q in the never-ending display of Things Karen Can't Quite Keep Up With:

The yard.

Sighing, I sent Kaitlyn in with all the packages, opened the garage door, and dragged out the little red mower I'd picked up for five bucks at a yard sale earlier in the summer. I think I'd used it once before assigning it to the very critical task of, oh, I don't know, weighting down the garage floor in case of a tornado or something.

Committed to taming the wilds before me, I revved up the motor and pushed off. Four inches later the blades clogged and the engine sputtered and died. Apparently my grass was way too tall for a single pass with my little Toro. I would have to raise the blades as high as they could go and mow the yard several times, lowering the blades a little each time.

I adjusted the blades and tried again. This time I went several feet before the little mower choked and died. I needed still more height. I knew bigger tires would help, but where could I possibly find the kind of tires I'd need to tame grass this high? I could only think of one place to get tires that big. Unfortunately, I'd misplaced my tire jack, and without it my Toyota 4Runner was just too heavy to lift. Clearly I'd just have to slog onward with what I had.

In midafternoon my neighbor Sharon ambled by with her dog, Gypsy, and stopped long enough to compliment my efforts.

A few hours later that same neighbor drove by in her car. She slowed and rolled down the window. "Still here?" she asked. I shrugged and told her I was committed to mowing my lawn twice a year whether it needed it or not.

By six o'clock I not only smelled like grass, sweat, and fuel, I was discouraged to boot. Even if I could get my lawn under control, what about the rest of my world? No wonder my chaotic lawn had felt familiar.

It mirrored my chaotic life. Into my mind kept popping the image of an overextended juggler sitting dazed on a psychiatrist's couch while mumbling, "So many balls, so few hands . . ."

The front door opened and Kaitlyn stepped onto the front porch. She stretched her back, taking a break from her own chores and homework, then took in the yard with a glance. "Wow!" she said admiringly.

I frowned. "It's still a mess. Look at that flower bed."

"You only think that because you're ankle deep in grass clippings. Come stand by me. From here it looks pretty good."

"Does it?" By then I had drafted my weed whacker into the fray. I paused and leaned on the handle. "Is it okay? Are *we* okay? You, me, and Kacie? Our lives now? I can't tell. Sometimes I feel so overwhelmed . . ."

"Mom, it's been almost a year. If we add that up for you, me, and Kacie, that comes to almost three years with no one else taking care of us."

I didn't quite follow the math, but I pretended I did.

Loyal Friend in Battle

History notes that Napoleon relied on chocolate for quick energy in his military campaigns.

M&M's were first sold in 1941 in cardboard tubes and quickly became a hit with American soldiers during World War II.

"Think about it," she continued. "The phone hasn't been turned off. We haven't starved. We've had electricity the entire time. The rent gets paid. The kitchen hasn't even been condemned yet."

I winced. "So we're doing okay?"

"*And* I got new clothes and new makeup. I'd say we're doing better than okay!" Kaitlyn flashed me a thumbs-up and disappeared back into the house.

I put down the weed whacker and kicked my way through the clippings and up the steps. Stepping onto the porch, I turned around, positioning myself carefully where Kaitlyn had been standing. I took a good, long look.

She had a point. From here it *did* look better. Not perfect. Still under the influence of chaos, still rough around the edges, still in transition, and still healing, but maybe not as hopeless as I'd thought.

Come stand by me.

I did, baby, I did. And it made all the difference in the world.

The View from Here

They say hindsight is twenty-twenty. But we don't have to wait until an experience becomes ancient history to improve our vision. Sometimes all it takes is a short walk. Or a fresh thought. Or a wise kid.

Perspective is wild, isn't it? I think it's fascinating that the exact same thing, when viewed from different directions, can look completely different. Imagine a sculpture of, say, actor Liam Neeson. In fact, let's cast him in character as that dashing Scottish hero from Liam's movie *Rob Roy*. Viewing our statue from one direction, we see Liam's imposing profile. A long shot shows off his stature and the confident way he's standing. Change our direction and distance and we're captivated by his unassuming smile and gentle eyes. Back here his flowing locks and broad shoulders are the stars. Looking up from here we see past the hem of his kilt and . . . never mind.

My point is that it's easy to walk around a statue. Or a house or a car or even a mountain. From a distance that mountain range looks daunting. Up close you can see the path up the face and then the crevice that signifies the mouth of the pass. From the other side, you see meadows. The guy in the helicopter sees it all at the same time.

Unfortunately, it's not so easy to take a stroll around a broken heart. Or personality conflicts at the office. Or a husband's suspicious computer viewing habits. What about financial stress? Anger issues? Those nagging painful memories? What about the fact that your parents are splitting up or your best friend has cancer or your thirty-two-year-old son wants to move back home? What about those extra thirty-five pounds? Or the fact that Rogaine for women can take months to reap noticeable improvements? And try as I might, I couldn't find a single helicopter pilot offering bird's-eye views of depression or divorce or the fact that your fourteen-year-old just got her tongue pierced. And let's not even *mention* softer jawlines or the way the backs of our hands are starting to sport that eye-catching crepey look.

Sheesh. I need chocolate after just *writing* that last paragraph.

Here's what I think. I think it's easy for you and me to get stuck in "default perspective mode." DPM occurs when the *first* way we look at something going on in our lives is the only way we ever see it. But let's cheat a little and refer to it as "default insight mode" just so I can call it DIM for short. This way I can say things like, "Being DIM-sighted might be convenient, but it sure doesn't give us a lot of options in life."

And it doesn't.

I don't know about you, but I'm tired of being DIM. Lately I've been trying to train myself to see every event or situation in my life from three or four different angles. That way I can pick through the bunch and select the healthiest perspective, the one I *really* want to embrace.

Here's what I've come up with so far.

New Perspective #1: Borrow the Eyes of a Friend

I love that Kaitlyn let me borrow her eyes for a fresh look at my lawn and life. "*Come stand by me.*" What an amazing gift that can be!

What if we got in the habit of asking our wiser friends and family, "From where you stand, how does this look? When you look at this situation in my life, what do *you* see?" We just might be surprised at how much their perspective differs from our own. After all, the story told by Little Red Riding Hood will never sound one bit like the story told by Grandma, whose story will never sound anything at all like the story told by Wolf, even if Grandma *did* get the inside scoop.

New Perspective #2: Borrow the Eyes of a Caricature Artist

No one understands the art of exaggeration quite like a caricature artist! Imagine making a living by finding small flaws and blowing them out of proportion. We laugh when an artist whips together a cartoon of a husband or friend or even ourselves.

Can an exaggerated perspective benefit us in other ways as well?

So last week I racked up nearly three hundred dollars in bounced check fees. *Three hundred dollars!* It's humiliating. I'm only telling you because we're such good friends, so please keep it under wraps. I'd feel really embarrassed if this got around.

I immediately went DIM. My initial response was to lash inward and call myself all sorts of unpleasantries, *irresponsible* and *stupid* being among the bunch. When I started telling myself things like *You shouldn't even be allowed to have a checkbook*, I wondered what would happen if I exaggerated my perspective and took the whole self-flagellation thing up a notch.

If I wasn't grown-up enough to handle a checkbook, what else wasn't I mature enough to handle? Driving a car? How about drinking coffee? Maybe I should turn in my Starbucks card and settle for something a little more maturity-appropriate, maybe one of those candy pacifiers. Definitely my spending needed to be leashed. Maybe I should be put on leash restriction, just like I put my Boston terrier on leash restriction for peeing around the house. Buddy's not allowed anywhere by himself anymore, at least until we get the peeing thing under control. If he's not in his kennel, I'm walking around the house with him tied to my belt loop. And when I'm tired of tripping over him, I drop his leash over the pointy ear of the griffin statue next to the couch in my living room. That should be me, leashed to the griffin statue for fiscal mismanagement, sucking on a Ring Pop, maybe even wearing a disposable diaper for good measure.

I thought about that image for a couple minutes, then shrugged and said, "Nah, it was just eleven bounced checks. Don't do it again."

As you can see, this approach works. Of course, if you don't have the time or energy to overreact with this kind of extended embellished self-flagellation, you can always take a shortcut and claw at your face and scream, "*Ohmigosh, we're all gonna die!*"

This works too.

New Perspective #3: Keep Moving, There's Nothing to See Here

My natural tendency hasn't always been to seek out the most reasonable and healthy perspective. Normally I panic.

After my marriage ended and I found myself living on my own, I woke up every morning scared. This went on for close to a year. My clock radio would blare, and I'd slap it silent and then begin the process of collecting the threads of yesterday's thoughts, which lay scattered on the edge of my consciousness, kind of like last night's discarded clothing. And always, as I grappled with that laundry pile of the morning's first thoughts, I'd experience an overwhelming sense of panic. *What am I doing alone? What if I can't do this, can't keep all the balls in the air? What if I drop something, like paying the mortgage or winterizing the sprinklers or renewing the car registration or making that orthodontist appointment for Kacie?*

Within fifteen minutes I'd have sorted through the pile of wrinkled thoughts and found something brave and presentable to put on for the day. You know, like when you've been laid up for a week with the flu and you realize you have twenty minutes to get to the bank to make that deposit (or you're going to bounce eleven checks) and you ransack your closet for any semi-clean, brightly-colored jacket you can throw over your sweat-stained, scary-smelling clothes so you can go out in public without being arrested. Like that.

Most days I gussied up enough to fool everyone around me and even myself. But those first waking moments were another story.

One morning I had had enough. I woke up, looked around at my piles of soiled scary thoughts, squared my jaw, and said, "It's laundry day, *bay*-bee!" It was time for some serious inventory.

A tasty sample from
The Chocolaphile Files

"My secret stash of chocolate is in the form of Ghirardelli 60 percent cocoa chocolate chips. It's amazing how fast a few at a time, ten times a day, can make a whole bag disappear when I'm in need of a little chocolate. It's just a tiny little chip. *Right!*"

Eileen Somers

I checked my health. Good.

I checked the roof over my head. Still there.

I checked my kids. Doing great.

I checked the fridge. Not only was there food in there, the bulb went on, so my electric bill was probably paid.

I checked my friendships. People still returned my calls, so that was a good sign.

My finances reminded me of a brand new face-lift—stretched but adjusting—but that was okay.

I checked my heart. Healing.

Could I put my finger on anything worth panicking over?

Nope. Hmmm. Interesting.

One day my friend Linda and I talked about this very thing while taking our dogs for a walk. She said, "Sometimes I get this looming feeling that something's wrong, that disaster is waiting around the corner. I can't always even put a finger on it. It's just a sense that I'm not okay, life isn't okay, everything's not okay."

I know exactly what she's talking about, and when I ask other women about it, *they* know what she's talking about too. Sometimes I wonder if that feeling is a ghost image from the last time something really *was* wrong in our lives, from seasons when disaster really *did* lurk. Maybe someone we loved was dying, or we knew we were about to lose a job, or things were turning terminally ugly in a once-beautiful relationship. Maybe we were in an abusive, critical environment and could be attacked at any moment. My point is, there *are* seasons in our lives when things aren't okay. Disaster really looms. The feeling is justified.

But sometimes I think our emotions are merely in a rut. We're fighting paper tigers. Mistaking windmills for giants.

So lately, when that feeling hits, I've been trying something new. I tell myself, "Take stock. Examine your health, finances, kids, relationships, deadlines, whatever. If something's *really* wrong, fix it. If not, that 'looming feeling' doesn't mean anything. It's a mirage. Empty. Nothing there."

Like a cop at a crime scene, I tell myself, "Move along. Keep moving. There's nothing to see here."

New Perspective #4: Wink

Do you remember the first time you discovered that by closing first one eye and then the other, you could make the room shift slightly from left to right? Or how when you close one eye and keep it closed, everything looks pancake flat, even though you know it's not?

I'm hardly surprised when I get two different perspectives from two different people. But I never cease to be amazed when I get two different perspectives from my own eyeballs. And it's not that hard. All I have to do is wink.

Roughly fifteen years ago my husband and I owned a fourplex in California. When his career moved us from California to Texas, we decided to keep the fourplex and try to manage it long distance.

Pretty soon, whenever the phone rang, I cringed. If a water heater leaked, I felt like a failure, as if a better landlord than me could have somehow averted the emergency. I felt the same way if my tenants got behind on rent, as if their inability to handle finances was a reflection of my value as a human being. From where I stood, the entire experience looked and felt like a fiasco. On a scale of one to ten, this was definitely a ten-doughnut binge in the making. And on a monthly basis no less! After several years (imagine what ten doughnuts a month can do over several years!), Larry and I got fed up and sold the property. And because we weren't willing to consider reinvesting our earnings back into real estate, a huge chunk of it went to the IRS.

Several years later, my mom told me a story from the days she and my dad were first starting to invest in commercial properties. One of their three buildings had been vacant for about six months, leaving them in a financial vise grip. My aunt was worried about my parents and told my mom as much.

My mom said, "Don't worry, Jeanette. We'll get it rented. And until we do, yes, it's a problem, but it's actually a *good* problem to have—it means we have investment properties! Do you realize how many people would love to own a second property and never will?" Not long after that conversation, my folks rented that building to a man who imported rice. He rented from them for many years and eventually bought the building for two and a half times what my folks had originally paid.

Sure, it's a problem, but it's a good problem to have.

Wow. I love that! If you ask me, that's a pretty freeing way to look at most any kind of problem! And it's surprisingly easy to do. Almost as easy as winking.

I'm back in the landlord business again with one little rental house. And, yeah, there are frustrations. But I'm honestly trying hard not to look at the frustrations as *problems* per se. Or if I do see them as problems, I try to remember that they're the *good* kind.

For example, eighteen months ago a tenant moved out of my little house. He was an airline pilot, a nice guy, but boy, was he messy! When I discovered a leak behind one of the toilets, the plumber I hired had to crouch behind a very filthy toilet to repair the leak. Pipe wrench in hand, he spoke freely about the evils of owning rentals.

"This is such a hassle," he said, waving the wrench around. "See? This is exactly why I won't own a rental. I don't want to deal with this stuff."

The thought crossed my mind, *But you* are *dealing with it. We're both dealing with it. The difference is, you're getting forty bucks an hour and I own the place.*

What problems are *you* facing today? Are they the normal glitches that accompany the privileges of success, parenting, employment, long life, love, and marriage? If so, try closing one eye and focusing on the privilege instead of the problem. See? It helps, doesn't it? And all it took was a wink.

New Perspective #5: Sometimes You Can't Believe Your Own Eyes

I want to talk about one last perspective. It's a perspective we're all familiar with, although if you're like me, you tend to forget it's there just when you need it the most.

I was reminded of this perspective the other day. My mom and I were sitting at McDonald's enjoying fish sandwiches and coffee when she told me a story.

She began by asking, "You know the petit point French provincial chair in my bedroom? The one I never let anyone sit on? Your great-grandmother Zaroi did the petit point on that chair. She'd sit for hours in the living room stitching one design or another, like that beautiful fireplace screen your uncle Steve has now. As a kid, I didn't think much about it—I just loved watching her. Now whenever I look at that chair or any of her handiwork, I'm reminded of that familiar illustration about the tapestry. You know how it goes, right? As the weaver works, he sees his design from the top side of the cloth and it's beautiful, while anyone watching him sees only the underside of the cloth and it's a mess, a jumble of threads and loose ends and ugly knots. But trust the weaver long enough and one day you'll get to see his handiwork from the other side, and it's gorgeous, with beautiful streams and trees and young lovers sitting on the bank."

I know the chair and the fireplace screen she's describing. There really *are* beautiful streams and trees and young lovers sitting on the bank.

Mom was reminding me of a perspective I don't seek nearly enough. It's called faith, and it's been described as the substance of things hoped for and the evidence of things not seen (see Heb. 11:1). It's the viewpoint of the Master Weaver at work, and for me to embrace *this* perspective, sometimes I have to ignore what my own eyes are telling me.

I'm going to try to look at my life from this perspective more often. Maybe you could do the same. After all, if Zaroi's handiwork is beautiful, can you imagine what the Master Weaver can do?

Living the Sweet Life

- Do you ever panic or overreact to something, eat wildly and out of control, then take a second look and realize things aren't as bad as you thought? When that happens, do you usually beat yourself up about it or make a mental note to try a different approach next time?

- Do you have people in your life you think are wise? People whose perspective you feel you can trust? The next time you feel DIM, what would happen if you asked one of these folks for his or her perspective on the matter?

- It's possible that someone whose wisdom you really trusted—maybe a parent or grandparent—is no longer here to give you advice. Think of something you wish you could ask them about. Now ask yourself what they would say to you if they could. What came to mind?

- When you want to see something from God's perspective, what works for you?

6

Community

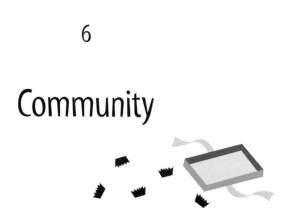

We've all been warned that the light at the end of the tunnel is probably the headlight of an oncoming train. And you know those moments when your life almost feels calm? I don't want to be a pessimist here, but can you say "eye of the storm"?

I had just come through a very stressful time in my life, and boy, was I ready for some calm. A lot of my stress came from the fact that about a year earlier I had started a little property management company. My husband and I had always owned a rental or two, so when I came across a few real estate investors in need of someone to manage their properties, I thought, "Hey, I've managed our rentals for years, why not manage theirs too?"

Apparently I never stopped to answer my own question. Within six months I was responsible for two fourplexes, six condos, and five houses. Between advertising fliers, leasing contracts, rent checks, and invoices from plumbers and handymen, paperwork overtook my house. My phone rang off the hook. With my life turned completely upside down, it finally dawned on me to answer the question I had neglected to answer earlier. The "why not?" was actually pretty simple: because people who hate managing their own houses, paperwork, and finances should avoid going into business managing *lots* of houses, paperwork, and finances for other people.

After a successful if stressful year, I sold my little business, put my cell phone on mute, and took a deep, cleansing breath. I had overdosed on chaos, and now it was time to embrace some calm. As far as I was concerned, I'd be eternally grateful if I never had to speak with a plumber or handyman again in my life. Fantasizing about simplifying my life, I gazed around my 1600-square-foot tract home and imagined myself planted happily in a two-room apartment.

About that time my friend Linda and I found ourselves in her Chrysler, cruising north on Interstate 25. We'd

> **A tasty sample from**
> ## The Chocolaphile Files
>
> "My predilection for dark chocolate came from my sister climbing into a high cupboard and sneaking into the baking chocolate when we were little kids and feeding it to me while I was sitting in my high chair."
>
> Barbara Faust

been friends for nearly twenty years; she'd recently moved to Denver and now lived two miles from me. We'd just spent the day with my family in Colorado Springs and were starting the drive back home when she said wistfully, "It's so beautiful here! Let's sell our houses and move to the Springs. We're both writers; we can live anywhere we want. We could buy houses close to your folks and Michelle and Gabriella. It would be fun! Let's do it!"

For several years I had dreamed about moving an hour south to Colorado Springs where my parents lived, as well as my sister and her little girl. Linda was right. It would be fun. And practical too. My sister worked nights as a police dispatcher, meaning my folks were helping out a lot with my five-year-old niece, Gabriella. If I lived closer, Gabriella could spend some nights with me as well. It was an enticing fantasy, but at the moment all I could think about was recuperating from my recent foray into free enterprise.

"Someday," I said matter-of-factly. "But there's no way I can make a move right now. Maybe in a couple years when Kacie starts junior high, but definitely not now."

A couple months later I came down with some weird flu-like virus. I ran a fever for two weeks, and when it finally broke, I was surprised to discover that I'd gone and bought a house in the Springs.

A Funny Thing Happened on the Way to the Medicine Cabinet

To the best of my recollection, here's how it unfolded: Shortly after my conversation with Linda, Kaitlyn left for college. And as if that weren't enough of a loss, a few weeks after *that* Linda landed this killer job in Florida. No, the Godfather wasn't involved, but it was still an offer she couldn't refuse. The morning her moving van pulled out of town, my fever was in full force, making it doubly easy to feel sorry for myself. And why shouldn't I have a pity party? My best friend was on her way to Florida. My teenager only came home on weekends. Sure, I'd wanted to downsize, but this was ridiculous. Feeling lousy and still sporting a temperature, I logged onto the Internet and found a house for sale in Colorado Springs. Before I knew it, I'd called the agent and made an appointment to see the house the next day.

My mom and sister went with me. Unfortunately, the little woodsy cottage that had looked so cozy and, well, downsized on the Internet turned out to be bigger and in need of *way* more repair than I'd thought. It definitely wasn't for me. I thanked the real estate agent for her time and reassured myself it was probably for the best. House hunting had been a fun diversion from fever and Florida-bound friends, but the fact remained that Kacie and I were settled in Denver and probably needed to stay there.

The agent returned the keys to the lockbox, and we turned to leave. As we crossed the gravel driveway, my mom gestured and said, "There's a house for sale across the street. Do you think we can get in to see it?"

One quick phone call and we were in the front door. Mom fell in love with the house immediately. "It's beautiful!" she said to me. "You should buy it!"

I shook my head. It *was* beautiful. And from what I could tell, it was priced way below market. But a thirty-six-year-old, three-story house in the woods was a far cry from my tract home in the city and an even more distant yodel from my vision of an even simpler abode. Kacie and I would rattle around in all that space!

On a whim I turned to my sister. "Hey, Shell, what do you say I get this place and you find a tenant for your house and move in too?"

From Lowly Beans to Decadent Confections

Cocoa beans go through a whole lot of sunning, sorting, and squeezing before chocolate dazzles your taste buds. Chocolate starts out as olive-sized beans removed from tropical-climate cacao trees. It takes about four hundred beans to make one pound of chocolate.

Once the cream-colored beans are harvested, they are fermented, sun drenched, sorted, cleaned, and roasted, giving them a swarthy look and a rich chocolate aroma. The beans are then shelled to expose their inner pure chocolate called a nib. The nibs are ground, squeezed, and crushed to produce chocolate liquor (sorry, it's nonalcoholic), cocoa butter, and cocoa powder.

Now the fun begins! Depending on the type of chocolate to be made, sugar, milk powder, and other ingredients are added. This mixture is aerated, heated, cooled, and formed into chunks, chips, bars, and more for eating. Just slip these tantalizing chocolates into their wrappings and they are ready for your cupboard, purse, desk drawer, or personal hidden stash.

So that's how it happened that by the time my fever broke, I had acquired a four-thousand-square-foot house. Not to mention a five-year-old.

All of us girls—Michelle, Gabriella, Kaitlyn, Kacie, and I—moved into our new digs thirty days later. As I write this, we've been here all of three months and my head's still spinning. I have yet to find the box with my printer cables, and there's not a single VCR hooked up quite right. For the third time in my life, there are Barbies in the stairwell and sippy cups on the kitchen counter. And as for handymen and plumbers? All I can say is thank goodness for speed dial. In the past ninety days we've had to replace one toilet, tear down a wall, replace a sink, and have the carpet restretched and steam cleaned after the boiler flooded the basement.

Did I simplify my life? Not unless before this move I was an air traffic controller who was managing the Waldorf-Astoria and running for public office in her spare time!

If Two's Company and Three Is ... Aw, Who's Counting Anyway?

You wouldn't know it by my lifestyle, but I believe in calm. And in solitude. And in the restorative qualities of silence. Really, I do. I'm well aware that at times the best things we can do for ourselves are isolate, downsize, and regroup. Even the Good Book assures us there's a time for everything under heaven, including "a time to embrace and a time to refrain" (Eccles. 3:5 NIV).

Apparently this was my time to embrace.

I say this because I'm now living five minutes from my aunt Jeanette (better known as Aunt Trick), two miles from my parents, and one staircase from my sister Michelle. Gabriella and Kaitlyn share the bedroom next to mine, although on any given night Gigi, Kacie, or Kaitlyn will have talked me into letting them sleep in my king-sized bed with me. And with a little luck my sister Renee, her husband Harald, and their boys Connor, Hunter, and Isaac will be moving here in a few months as well.

I thought I needed peace and quiet. Instead, I'm immersed in community, which is all right by me because, honestly, the longing to be a part of a healthy, happy community is something we all share. It's why we fell in love with the Waltons and even Mike and Carol Brady and all their groovy kids.

Of course, you don't have to do what I did and follow in the stiletto steps of the Carringtons and the Ewings by embracing the multifamily commune motif. You can do other things to create a greater sense of community in your life. Just today I had lunch with a friend who told me about three things she's doing to expand her community: attending a weekly book group, joining a singles fellowship at her church, and signing up for a softball league.

I like her approach. Connecting with new friends is a tried and true way to beef up the sense of community in your life. Make enough new friends and you'll definitely be busy. There's also the chance that you'll really hit it off with someone or even a small group of folks. That's when the power of community *really* kicks in—when the people in your world become more than movie pals, pew partners, and work buddies and start becoming best friends, mentors, soul mates, and even lifelines.

Of course, another way to quench our craving for community is to find ways to connect more authentically with people we already know and like. Maybe even people we love.

Strange Brood

I hadn't lived in the same city as my original family for fifteen years. And the last time we shared a kitchen or bathroom? I shudder to name the year. I thought I knew these people pretty well, but when you really think about it, we'd been living parallel lives for more than a decade, intersecting on weekends and holidays and via email and cell phones. Now that we're spending more time together, I'm learning new things all the time about the people I've known all my life.

For instance, I had no idea my mom is addicted to McDonald's fish sandwiches. Or that my dad would give his eyeteeth for an empty mayonnaise jar he can wash out and use to store workshop doodads. Or that Michelle is so good at sticking to schedules and goals and avoiding the kinds of extraneous whims and rabbit trails that seem to define her older sibling. And I'm thoroughly enjoying discovering the things everyone is passionate about,

"Giving chocolate to others is an intimate form of communication, a sharing of deep, dark secrets."

Milton Zelman, publisher of "Chocolate News"

like Mom's excitement over the event center she and Dad have started. It's fun to be reminded of how much she has always loved the various business ventures—some have been more *adventures* than ventures—that they have launched through the years.

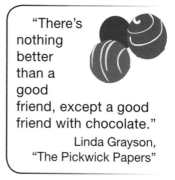

"There's nothing better than a good friend, except a good friend with chocolate."
Linda Grayson,
"The Pickwick Papers"

Of course, they're learning new things about me too.

I know it's easy to assume we know everything there is to know about the people who have been in our lives for a long time. The phrase "two ships passing in the night" doesn't refer only to acquaintances or strangers. We can cruise carelessly past people we love as well, neglecting to take the time to drop anchor, pull on diving gear, and explore the unseen treasures of the souls of those closest to us. And then we wonder why we feel alone and adrift—regardless of the number of people we meet or think we know.

If you ask me, it's easy to make this mistake with family and friends but even easier to make it with our spouses. A scene in the movie *Runaway Bride* comes to mind. You know the plot, right? In a desperate bid to save his career, New York columnist Ike Graham spends a couple weeks shadowing Maggie Carpenter, observing her oddest quirks, mining her deepest thoughts, and falling in love with her in the process. The scene that always gets me is when the evolving Graham finds himself in a conversation with his ex-wife Ellie in which

he asks thoughtfully, "What went wrong? Did I just
. . . not see you?"

She appears to answer as kindly as she can. "No.
No, you didn't."

"I'm sorry," he says. "I'm sorry."

In the end Richard Gere's character learns his lesson,
winning Maggie's heart by seeing her so clearly that he
comes to know her even better than she knows herself.

Okay, so it's just a movie, and we all know that Richard
Gere's Ike was destined to hook up with Julia Roberts's
Maggie. But what if he had learned his lesson the first time
around? What if he hadn't cruised blindly past the first
woman he swore to love for a lifetime? If he had observed
her quirks and explored *her* heart on an ongoing basis,
would their marriage have lasted? Would their love story
have been the one with the romantic happy ending?

What about you and me?

We crave connection and community. It's easy to believe that the best way to enjoy these things is to get to
know new people. I'm wondering what would happen if
we got to know "old" people, as in the folks we *already*
know. What if you and I identified a handful of people
currently in our lives and decided to discover something
new about them on a weekly basis? What if we looked
for endearing oddities, inquired about their childhood,
or sought to understand their point of view? What if we
mined their wisdom, forgave their flaws, or cherished
their quirks? What if we asked them to tell us three
things about themselves we didn't already know?

The next time you're stressed out by crisis, change,
or chaos in your world, go ahead: Simplify your life.

Streamline your stressors. Downsize your house. But keep your world brimming with authentic connections with a community of people you love and know. Really know. And as you're getting to know these folks, if you find anyone who's good with tools, pass along my number, will you?

I figure a girl can never know too many handymen or plumbers.

Living the Sweet Life

- Let's talk about people in your life right now. Do you have any healthy relationships with people you'd love to get to know better? Do you have any relationships with toxic or "bad influence" people you should probably spend less time with?

- How can you enlarge your community? Attend church? Join a small group? Participate in a book club? Volunteer? (If you're single, check out www .singlevolunteers.org to meet other singles while helping various charities and nonprofits in your neighborhood.) What other ideas can you come up with?

- To discover new things about the friends and family you already know and love, try the little game we talked about in chapter 2. Ask them to tell you twenty-one things about themselves . . . and then listen. *Really* listen.

7

Context

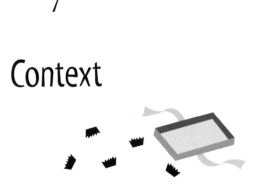

The original plan wasn't complicated at all.

I was supposed to leave my house at 4:45 in the morning, pick up my friend Cathy Schwartz at her house, drive to the airport, drop her off near her gate, park my car, then get to my gate. We had different destinations—Cathy was catching a plane to Ohio to visit her daughter, and I was on my way to Florida to visit my friend Linda—but with our flights less than an hour apart, we figured carpooling would be fun.

And it would have been even *more* fun if getting to airports on time—heck, getting *anywhere* on time—weren't such a problem for me.

I've been chronically late all of my life, although for years I had an excuse: I was never *completely* sure what time it was. After all, some clocks run slow. Some clocks run fast. Batteries die. Cities have power failures. Sometimes you plain ol' forget to pay your electric bill. My point is, if you simply glance at a strange clock—a clock you haven't lived with for years, a clock whose battery life and idiosyncrasies are unfamiliar to you—how can you know what time it is *really?* And don't *even* get me started on Daylight Savings Time. This is why—between variances in power sources and Daylight Savings Time snafus—I'm comfortable assuming that any given clock at any given time is probably inaccurate by up to several hours either direction, so why sweat it?

You can get around this problem, but you have to be religious about several conditions: First, you can only trust clocks in your own home that are atomic clocks *and* are powered by a wall adapter plus battery backup. These clocks receive satellite transmissions that sync them daily with the official U.S. atomic clock in Boulder, Colorado, a clock which is *still* not foolproof since it can gain or lose up to one second over thirty million years but seems to be reliable other than that. You also have to make sure the Daylight Savings Time button on your new household atomic clock is turned to "On." If it's not, you can still be on time to work, but only if you are commuting to parts of Arizona.

The night before Cathy and I were to ride together to the airport, I was thankful that I had followed all these rules to a T. In fact, several years ago I spent an obscene amount of money at Walgreens buying atomic clocks for every room in my house. By all accounts, my time-related dilemmas should have been ancient history—which is exactly why the next part of my story makes no sense at all.

Time Flies—or Not

The morning of my flight I woke before dawn, ran through the shower, grabbed the clothes I wanted to take with me, and tossed them on the bed next to my suitcase. Since I hate returning home to a messy house, I decided to take a minute to Windex my bathroom countertop and mirror. I was standing in my bra and panties doing this very thing when I happened to glance at the atomic clock positioned strategically in my bathroom, saw the numbers four five nine, thought to myself, "Oh, look, I'm supposed to be pulling into Cathy's driveway exactly one minute from now," then continued calmly Windexing the mirror.

I kept Windexing the mirror.

There wasn't any internal alarm. No mad dash to throw clothes onto my body and into my suitcase. No urgent desire to fling myself out my front door. Just a casual observation, the unjustifiable feeling that since she wasn't expecting me for another minute, I *could* technically

> **A tasty sample from**
> **The Chocolaphile Files**
>
> "I'm getting better at identifying the real reason I'm eating. Usually it's a combination of low blood sugar and unmet emotional needs. . . . Now that I'm a diabetic, food is a project for me—I have to plan to eat on a schedule. . . . If I eat outside that schedule, I will eventually ask myself, 'What's up? Why am I eating?' . . . Dark chocolate in particular tends to halt my 'hunt' for chocolate. Then I get to face why I'm 'hunting' in the first place, which often turns into an interesting conversation between God and me."
>
> Charlene Bruno

still make it on time, and then the *queek queek* of the moist paper towel against the mirror.

I won't describe the next couple hours to you. Suffice it to say that I barely made my flight. The only reason I got on the plane at all is because I asked Cathy to drive so I could leap from the moving car to curbside check-in and then sprint the rest of the way to my gate. Running at such a fast clip must have jarred some details loose in my brain, because somewhere en route I realized that when I returned to Colorado, my car would be waiting for me in long-term parking, where Cathy was at that very moment turning off the ignition and reaching for her duffle bag, but the *keys* to that car would be with Cathy in Ohio.

Needless to say, I felt pretty frazzled as I boarded my plane, clicked my seat belt together, and settled back for the flight. I knew in the next day or two I'd have to solve the dilemma of the keys, but I couldn't do anything about it at that very moment. Eventually I calmed down enough to turn to the stack of paperwork I carry with me anytime I travel.

Something about reading and working on planes always appeals to me. I get a lot done. Maybe it's because there's no one I know to talk to, my phone is off-limits, I can't check my email, and I can't even distract myself by going to the fridge. Who knew being strapped in a chair for three hours could work out so well for me?

The first item on my agenda was a stack of research I'd printed off the Internet. My sister had sent me foraging online for information on adult ADD. She said some stuff she'd read reminded her of me. It could be interesting.

I might even do an article on the topic at some point in the future. I grabbed a pink highlighter and dug in.

Twenty minutes later tears were streaming down my face.

Now It All Makes Sense

What did I know about attention deficit disorder in adults? As I mined the stack of articles before me, I kept expecting to read stories of former ten-year-old boys who couldn't sit still in school. Instead I found pages and pages of information about men and women experiencing the exact same setbacks, challenges, questions, feelings, and wounds that seemed at times to dominate my life.

The pages described everything about me, from the paperwork on my kitchen table to the number of speeding tickets I get to the way I always think I can do *one last thing* before I head out the door. Clutter, procrastination, distraction—all present and accounted for. I found a great article explaining why my kids seem to feel the need to set oven timers so I'll remember to pick them up from school. I found a detailed description of the exact items in the mountains of junk in my garage—right next to what looked like a direct quote from my banker on the late fees I always pay because I put off paying my

"Make a list of important things to do today. At the top of your list, put 'eat chocolate.' Now, you'll get at least one thing done today."

Gina Hayes

bills even when I have money in my account.

After reading a paragraph on women who can't put things away where they belong because if something is "out of sight it's out of mind," I glanced horrified at the sunglasses, cell phone, and wallet laid out on the airplane seat next to me. I'd long given up carrying a purse for that exact reason: Why carry a purse when I had to dig through it every ten minutes to make sure the essentials I'd just tucked inside were still there? Keeping those wily items where I could see them at all times always seemed like a much better idea.

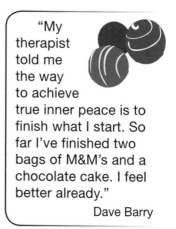

"My therapist told me the way to achieve true inner peace is to finish what I start. So far I've finished two bags of M&M's and a chocolate cake. I feel better already."

Dave Barry

But the final straw—the words that brought it all crashing home and opened floodgates of tears somewhere over Oklahoma—was the online post of a woman with ADD who wrote, "I can read the numbers on a clock, but it doesn't sink in. It's not that I don't care, it's that it doesn't seem to register with my brain. I just can't seem to develop a normal concept of time no matter how hard I try."

If I Only Had a Clue

Do you have stuff in your life that doesn't make sense, stuff that drives you nuts, stuff you seem to butt your head against over and over again without resolve until the only thing left for you to do is drive to Starbucks and drown your sorrows in a double-blended venti chocolate brownie Frappuccino?

Let's face it, sometimes we get stuck. One Christmas Kacie received a little toy dog who had risen to TV commercial stardom because he could walk and bark. Every time he took a step his toy motor whirred, and every three steps he emitted a squeaky little bark, meaning we got to listen to this incessant *whir whir whir SQUEAK whir whir whir SQUEAK* whenever Kacie played with him, which—since this was her *favorite* Christmas present of the bunch—she did religiously for two entire days. What the little fella couldn't seem to do was reverse, so every now and then I'd be in another room and hear *whir whir whir whir whir whir whir whir* with no *squeak* whatsoever, and I'd know that Fido had walked into a wall. Sure enough, there he'd be, nose to drywall, his little motor whirring and his little paws sliding endlessly back and forth on the linoleum, no momentum, no progress, no celebratory little squeaky bark.

I'm still haunted by the image.

It's probably because I empathize with Fido, having spent more time than I want to admit with my own nose against the wall, my little motor whirring vainly, my paws sliding back and forth without moving me one iota closer to answers I crave. You've been there too, haven't you?

The good news is that every now and then something stops us in our tracks and makes us back away from the tiny square of wall on which we've been focusing.

Looking up for the first time, we take in the whole wall, and then we broaden our sights to discover our wall is really just part of a room in a series of rooms, and we notice that right there—not more than six inches to the right of the solid surface at which we've been endlessly scratching— is a doorway.

That's what I felt like when I stumbled across information that helped me place my tendencies in the context of the larger world of adults with inactive attention deficit disorder—like after years of butting my head up against a wall, I'd just been shown the hallway leading all the way to the front door.

Sometimes a Little Information Goes a Long Way

I'll be the first to admit that these kinds of nagging problems send us regularly to the Pop-Tarts and Pringles. And yet sometimes the thing we need most—the thing we're craving deep inside—is not carbs but context. We stumble around, more than a little lost, studying the obstacles immediately before us and wondering why we're not getting anywhere. And yet if we could stop focusing on individual trees long enough to take a good look at the forest, we just might find our bearings and make it home.

Context is that thing that inspires us to smack our foreheads and say, "*Now* it all makes sense!"

It's the moment you realize the sugar-free fudgesicles you've been eating all month actually contain *more* calories than the regular ones.

It's the moment you realize you've been feeling so queasy and bloated because you're pregnant.

It's the revelation that you owed so much money to Apple last month because your teenager figured out the password to your iTunes account.

It's when someone finally tells you that your hunky unmarried coworker is gay.

Aha! she says.

Fifteen years ago I couldn't seem to stop feeling numb and sad—until a doctor diagnosed clinical depression and gave me the information I needed to get well again.

Until six months ago, I kept bumping up against a wall of frustration over chaos and procrastination—until a stack of articles gave me the information I needed to restrategize my life.

When my niece Gabriella was three weeks old, a thumbprint-sized red birth mark on her neck began to swell and spread. Michelle took Gabriella to a number of pediatricians, but no one could explain or solve the

Who Invented Chocolate Anyway?

About 4,000 years ago, Central and South American Indians discovered the savory delights of cocoa. These ancient peoples—including the Aztecs and Mayas—mixed cocoa with all sorts of stuff including chili peppers and honey to make a spicy drink called "chocolatl." They must have truly enjoyed the drink, because the botanical name of chocolate is *Theobroma cacao*, which means "god food." They were convinced chocolate was the nectar of the gods, and of course many of us feel the same way today!

problem. Within weeks Gabriella's "birthmark" covered one side of her neck and half of her face up to her ear. Even scarier, her face and throat had swollen to three times their normal size. Apparently this problem was *not* going away by itself, and Michelle and her husband Russ were beside themselves—until Michelle's online research led her to Milton Waner, a New York doctor specializing in the treatment of a benign but aggressive blood tumor called a hemangioma. Today all traces of Gabriella's hemangioma are gone, and my niece is a vivacious five-year-old with a beautiful complexion.

Sometimes the thing we need in order to see our problem in context and get it solved is *information*. With the right details, suddenly we know exactly what to do. The solution we couldn't even imagine now seems within our grasp.

Information Solves, Understanding Heals

Of course, sometimes a problem isn't something we need to solve as much as something we need to salve. We don't need *how-to* as much as *healing*.

When her son died from AIDS, my friend Pat found herself crashing into pain and unanswered questions everywhere she turned.

Another friend, Cheryl, can't seem to stop her heart from spinning endlessly over dead-end questions about a relationship that went bust.

When Linda's dad was dying, she traveled to California to tell him she loved him. Would he say he loved her back? Or that he was proud of her? Or any of the other things he had never managed to communicate to her in fifty years? Right before Linda arrived, her dad slipped into a coma. She spent four days at the side of a man who—no matter how much he might have wanted to—would never say the things she needed so desperately to hear.

We can get stuck on this stuff too. Stuff we can't fix or change or avoid. No do-overs here. To get unstuck, we still crave context. Something that makes us go *Aha.* An insight that allows us to finally exhale some of the hurt and pain and say, "Okay. All right. I can start to make a little sense of it all."

Pat told me that seeing her son's journals turned into a book helped her heal. "His death had a purpose. People have been helped. It enabled me to start making sense out of an otherwise senseless loss."

Cheryl couldn't fix the breakup that broke her heart. Even learning that clinical depression had contributed to some of her boyfriend's erratic behavior couldn't solve the problem at hand. But it did give her insight that helped her to heal and move on with her life.

Linda didn't get the resolution she sought in California. But she didn't come home empty-handed. "Sitting with my silent dad for four days, I had plenty of time to think. You always see your dad as someone bigger than life. But in those hours I came to see him as a man who had been hurt by his own parents, someone who probably did the best he could, someone whose own wounds made him incapable of recognizing the wounds he inflicted on others. The things I longed to hear remain unsaid. But I've made peace. I'm moving on."

Life Is Good

Shortly after I got home from my Florida trip, I was chatting with my dad at the kitchen table. My dad is my hero. A country boy from Kentucky, he starts companies, fights injustice, does million-dollar real estate deals, takes care of his family, *and* never meets a stranger in the process. He also has this endearing way with words.

So we're just sitting there, chewing the fat, when suddenly he says gently, "Your mom told me about that ADT thing."

"The alarm company?"

"Whatever it's called. And I want you to know you don't have it. You're okay. Everybody gets overwhelmed sometimes. Everybody loses their keys. That stuff happens to everyone. Don't accept any labels, baby. You're fine."

"Thanks, Dad." I ponder his words a moment, then say, "You're right, I *am* okay. And as far as labels go, maybe they apply to me and maybe they don't. I'm fine with it either way. All I know is there's information out there that, whatever it's called, has already given me some great ideas for managing all the exasperating details of life. I'm using bulletin boards to organize my bills now instead of file folders. I'm setting kitchen timers to create uninterrupted blocks of time so I can write or clean house or whatever. When I'm running late and get the urge to do one last thing, I know now it probably doesn't *really* have to be done right then. I remind myself that I *always* get that feeling and the only thing it means is that, well, I always get that feeling."

My house is still stocked with atomic clocks. I still think strapping myself into an airline seat for two hours makes me more productive. And even when I'm late, Cathy still wants to be my friend. I guess the good news is that some things never change.

The other good news is that some things do.

Living the Sweet Life

- Do you remember the parable of three blindfolded men describing an elephant? The one touching the elephant's leg swears the beast is like a tree. The man holding the trunk claims the elephant is like a serpent. The man grasping the tail swears the animal is just like a rope. Not one of these guys is going to get it right until he takes off his blindfold and sees the whole elephant at once. Have you ever done the same thing with a problem or wound in your life?

- Is something making you feel stuck right now? If so, would information or understanding help you get unstuck? Which one? How might you go about obtaining what you need to move on?

- Do you know how to find the resources you need? If not, is there someone you know who can help you figure it out? Do you have a trusted friend who is a whiz at researching things online? Would a pastor be a helpful link to good counselors in your area?

8

Viscosity

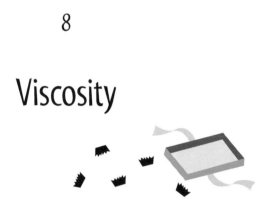

The hit of the bridal show was definitely the chocolate fountain.

Not that this should come as any surprise.

Imagine satin sheets of chocolate cascading so smoothly as to appear motionless. Visualize a seamless wall of glossy chocolate suspended tantalizingly in mid-air, right beside a huge bowl of ruby red strawberries.

Brides on their way to check out the booths of other vendors tried to walk nonchalantly past the chocolate fountain. More often than not they ended up captivated by the magical streaming chocolate. Inevitably these bright-eyed women would turn to their mothers or friends or fiancés and blurt, "And we're *definitely* having a chocolate fountain at the reception."

I was working at a booth in the next aisle, so for the first hour or so I only got to observe the fountain and its worshipers from afar. My mom and dad had just launched the Citadel Event Center in Colorado Springs, and my job that afternoon was to hand out brochures, invite folks to visit our facilities, and enter names in a drawing to be held at our grand opening in a couple weeks. Lots of women entered our drawing. Maybe it was because one of the prizes was the complimentary use of a chocolate fountain if they booked their event at our center.

Chocolate definitely seemed to be the theme of the day. Maybe that's why as soon as I got a break, I headed toward that fountain.

I never said I was too good to be seduced by chocolate.

Just like everyone else, I found myself enthralled by the way the chocolate flowed so flawlessly and sedately as to appear to be defying gravity. Since then I've learned the illusion is created by the viscosity—or thickness—of the chocolate. On that day I didn't care what the reason was. I was simply hypnotized by the motionless cascades of molten chocolate.

Whether I was transported by the waterfalls of cocoa or merely influenced by the ambiance of the bridal show, before long I found myself meandering down memory lane, remembering back when I was twenty-one and planning my own trip down the aisle.

"Never eat more than you can lift."
Miss Piggy

Truth be told, I'd felt like a princess in fairy tale. Of course, it *was* the summer of

1981 and Princess Diana's *real* fairy tale wedding was taking place three weeks before mine, so it was impossible to pick up a magazine or turn on the TV without being bombarded with news and images of royal romance. All the hoopla of *her* wedding might have made mine seem eclipsed in some fashion, but it didn't. It made my own future all the more magical, as if the promise of Diana's happily-ever-after made my happiness all the more likely as well.

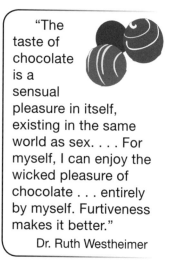

"The taste of chocolate is a sensual pleasure in itself, existing in the same world as sex. . . . For myself, I can enjoy the wicked pleasure of chocolate . . . entirely by myself. Furtiveness makes it better."

Dr. Ruth Westheimer

After all, weren't we dreaming of the same things? Lifelong love. Happiness. Emotional intimacy. Sexual passion. The rich patina that comes when you love the same person for a very long time. The miracle of learning to laugh again after disappointment or loss. All the babies we wanted. Stepping-stone problems instead of the millstone-around-your-neck kind of problems. Cascades of laughter. More laughter than tears. The kind of laughter that *brings* you to tears.

Chocolate fountain futures, that's what we wanted. Viscosity. Lives so thick with love and laughter that time almost stands still.

We know how the story ended for Diana. As for me, twenty-five years later, my ring finger is once again bare.

When my dad asked me to help work the booth at the bridal show, I wondered how I'd feel rubbing elbows with so many women all glowy and iridescent with prenuptial hopes and dreams. Would I find myself laughing *with* these love-struck optimists or *at* them?

At the close of the show, I still didn't have my answer. I wasn't sure how I felt about it all. I'd met a lot of optimistic brides. Were most of them destined for heartache and failure, or were chocolate fountain futures possible after all?

Two weeks later I awoke to an ice-glazed Saturday morning. It was the day of our grand opening at the Citadel Event Center. Kacie and I dressed as warmly as we could, bundled into my truck, and headed downtown to meet the rest of my family. We spent the next three hours preparing for the hordes of potential customers we hoped would be attending our open house. While I arranged a banquet table of finger foods, Kacie learned how to use the helium tank, inflating literally hundreds of balloons and managing to sound like Alvin the Chipmunk the entire time.

Our first couple arrived a little after noon. They really liked the place. They said they would book their reception with us as soon as they set the date for their wedding. At one point the bride-to-be turned to me and said, "I visited your booth at the bridal show and entered my name in the chocolate fountain drawing. Have you drawn the names yet?"

I said, "Not yet," and put out another plate of meatballs.

I wish I could say that hundreds of potential customers toured our facilities, but apparently even brides aglow with wedding fever are susceptible to black ice and subzero temperatures. Only one other couple made it to our open house, and they had already booked another venue for their wedding and reception.

In the late afternoon we closed and locked the doors. Dad, Mom, Kacie, and I sat exhausted around one of the tables and snacked on meatballs and cheese skewers, something that we were going to be doing for a very long time, judging from the mounds of untouched food.

Before long I'd had my fill of protein and upgraded to the other food group—namely the platter of chocolate chip cookies. Which is probably why I suddenly remembered the drawing.

"What's the plan?" I asked through a mouthful of Toll House. "Do we draw names now or what?"

"I guess not," Dad said. "The rules on the entry form said that you had to be present to win. No one's here."

"Dad, the open house lasted three hours. No one wants to hang around an open house for three hours. I think we should change the rules. Let's say anyone who showed up at the open house at all can win."

"That seems reasonable," my dad conceded.

"So should we draw names now?"

"Why? Who's eligible?"

"There was that first couple. They entered the drawing *and* showed up. They could win."

"So we have *one* eligible couple?" Dad laughed. "Karen, there's a hundred forms in that drum."

"But if we *did* draw their names, they could win, right?"

While we were still negotiating, Kacie walked over to the drum and gave it a healthy spin.

Dad grinned at me. "Okay, smarty-pants, do you even know the names of that first couple who came by?"

I glanced at a sheet of paper by my plate. It was the guest registry we'd placed by the front door. Seven people had signed in, including my entire family. It was easy to find the signature of our one eligible bride. I read the name.

At the exact same moment, Kacie and I said, "Emily Jackson."

I looked up at Kacie. She was reading the first and only entry form she'd pulled from the drum.

What Women Want

Here's one of my favorite conversations from the TV series *Gilmore Girls*.

LUKE: Uh, I made some brownies. I thought you might like some.

LORELAI: Oh, gee, since I just ate half a bag of marshmallows, six Pop-Tarts, four bagel dogs, and a really stale Cheese Nip—yup, it's brownie time, thanks.

LUKE: Well, I accidentally dropped triple the amount of cocoa powder in the batter, so I either had to dump the batch or find someone with some sort of superhuman chocolate tolerance—only one name came to mind.

LORELAI: I love being special.

Mom and Dad said it was a miracle. Of course, they've been happily married for forty-eight years and probably still believe in magic and maybe even Santa Claus. I, on the other hand, told Kacie to go back to the drum and make sure "Emily Jackson" wasn't written on all one hundred entry forms.

It wasn't.

Okay, so maybe it's possible after all. You know, chocolate fountain miracles. All that happily-ever-after stuff. Viscosity. A life so thick and rich with good stuff that time almost stands still.

We called Emily with the good news, then spent the next hour putting away food and washing dishes. In spite of the bad weather and poor turnout, this had been our first big event and really felt like a pretty great accomplishment. Mom and I teamed up to figure out how to clean our elaborate industrial punch fountain. We worked hard and laughed hard too. At one point I noticed she was glowing. Maybe it was the hot soapy water, but maybe it was just because we were having fun. My sister Michelle and her new boyfriend came by, which was great because Michelle seemed to be the only one of us who kept a level head when, for some reason unknown even to myself, I went to the popcorn maker and tilted the popping pan a mere 30 seconds after filling it, dumping kernels and cold oil all over the previous batches of freshly popped corn.

Later I heard squeals and peeked into the main auditorium to find Kacie and Gabriella engaged in some sort of balloon tag. And through it all my dad grinned and looked about twenty years younger than usual. It was probably because he's been trying to get us all back into some sort of family business ever since my sisters and I were in junior high and we all worked together in the family printing business, although you have to wonder why he's so anxious to repeat the experience considering Michelle once stapled her hand to the bottom of a cardboard box and I was caught, at fifteen, kissing our twenty-one-year-old pressman.

Late in the evening I bundled two exhausted girls into my 4Runner and headed home. Within a few blocks Kacie was sound asleep in the front seat and Gabriella had nodded off in the back. I was tired too, but thoughtful.

Yeah, sometimes I'm a skeptic, but the day's events had renewed my faith. Chocolate fountain lives really *are* possible. I know mine's turning out fine. I can only hope as much for Emily.

Living the Sweet Life

- Are you spending so much time lamenting what you *don't* have that you're missing out on what you do have? How often do you put your life on hold by thinking, "If only . . . then . . ."? If you're convinced a part of your life is on hold because you're not married or skinny or single or financially secure, think again. On second thought, stop thinking and start living. As in *today*.

- Remember the hymn that begins, "Count your blessings, name them one by one"? Consider this a pop quiz: Name ten things you're thankful for. Counting on fingers is encouraged. Please begin counting at the tone. Beeeeeep.

• Every time we go to the movies we see fictional characters enjoying the kinds of memory-rich moments that epitomize a life lived large and lived well: A moment of chemistry sparked by unexpected eye contact with a stranger across the room. Laughing with best friends over lunch. Hours spent burning the midnight oil to make an impossible dream come true. An overdue heart-to-heart with a parent or sibling. A pillow fight with the kids. Abandoning the dishes to dance with a spouse in the kitchen. The fight that almost ends a relationship—and the turning point that gives it a new beginning. What movie-moment memories have you experienced lately? Describe three. And if you can't think of any, make one tonight.

9

Sleep

Oh, great. I need to write a chapter on sleep and I'm going to have to stay up all night to do it.

Such is the nature of deadlines.

Heck, such is the nature of life.

I never had trouble getting a good night's sleep until I got pregnant and discovered that climbing out of bed every forty-five minutes to go to the bathroom can really put a damper on feeling rested the next morning. Not that I'm complaining. Spending my pregnancy with dark circles under my eyes was great training for motherhood, when uninterrupted sleep became the stuff of fantasies. When my babies were little, you could have offered me a night with Tom Selleck or an undisturbed night on a Simmons Beautyrest, and I would have sent Mr. Magnum packin'.

That was ten years ago. These days my postnatal cravings for shut-eye are a thing of the past. After all, my babies aren't babies anymore.

But that doesn't mean I'm getting enough sleep. A really good sign that I'm not getting enough sleep is that pile of Reese's Peanut Butter Cup wrappers next to my coffee cup.

Emotional eating gets all the press. But the truth is that there are *other* reasons you and I crave chocolate and Doritos in the kinds of quantities that make normal people, like Sumo wrestlers, push away from the table long before we do.

Sometimes the reason we binge has nothing to do with our emotions and everything to do with how well we slept last night.

Why Sleep? Because You'll Eat Less

A friend of mine from Georgia once complained, "I've been eating as hard as I can all day and I just can't get full." If you ask me, Alta's on to something.

Do you ever have days when you can't stop eating no matter how hard you try? Maybe you're not even hungry. Maybe your stomach feels stretched. But you just can't seem to stop the trough action, and you're not sure why.

It's possible that the hormones that are supposed to shut down your appetite aren't doing their job. Apparently sleep is nature's little appetite suppressant, and when we skimp on sleep, we can compromise our ability to feel full or know when to say when. Here's how it works.

A tasty sample from
The Chocolaphile Files

"God designed our bodies to tell us what we need, when we need it, and when we're satisfied. If we listened to those signals and counted on him for everything else, I believe we wouldn't have such a need to fill up that void inside."

Shelly Johnson

When you and I sleep less than six hours a night, we're hungrier the next day. This is because our sleep-deprived bodies produce less leptin. You are probably thinking the same thing I did: *leptin schmeptin*, which translates to "Who cares?" in Irish or "Whatev" in teenspeak.

Unfortunately, leptin is the blood protein that suppresses our appetites and also helps our brains know when we've had enough food. So when our sleep-deprived bodies produce less leptin, it means—to put it in concise medical terminology—*we never stop eating.*

And to make doubly sure we soon weigh more than our refrigerators, our sleep-starved bodies not only produce less leptin, at the same time they produce more grehlin, which is some sort of substance that makes us want to eat even *more.*

In other words, skimping on sleep tonight means tomorrow not only will you feel hungrier than normal, your body won't feel full (even when it is) and your brain won't send the signal to stop eating (even when it should).

Why Sleep? Because You'll Eat Healthier Things

So missing sleep makes us hungrier. As a late night kind of person, you can imagine how thrilled I was to hear *that* nasty little news flash. Still, I had to wonder . . . could I beat the system? What would happen if, the next time I stayed up late, I tried to satisfy all that amplified hunger with grilled chicken and cauliflower?

Nice try. Unfortunately, it turns out that missing sleep affects not only how much we crave but *what* we crave as well.

In one study a group of people slept four hours a night. After just two nights they not only lost leptin and gained grehlin, they also started craving foods high in sugar and starches. Researchers suspect that since our brains are fueled by glucose, sleepy brains go into some sort of distress mode, demanding extra glucose in the form of sugar and simple carbs that turn into sugar.

Not that it matters. What matters is that far more than you and I ever dreamed, our craziest food cravings and sleep patterns are linked.

Why Sleep? Because You'll Shrink Your Chances of Being Obese

I'd like to mention one more study, and it's a scary one. In lay terms, it says simply that people who sleep less have *much* greater odds of being fat. The study doesn't say why. Maybe it's that leptin/grehlin/brain thing we just talked about. Maybe it's because people who average four hours of sleep for even just a couple nights in a row show signs of insulin resistance, a condition that precedes diabetes and causes weight gain.

Whatever the reasons, if you average six hours of sleep a night, you are *23 percent more likely* to be obese than your neighbor who gets seven to nine hours of shut-eye.

If you sleep five hours a night, your chances go up to 50 percent.

If you average four hours of sleep a night, *your chances of becoming obese go up to 73 percent.*

Cuckoo for Cocoa Puffs or Desperately Seeking Snoozin'?

So how much sleep do we need? For our bodies to do the best job handling sugar, maintaining stable blood sugar levels, craving healthy foods, feeling full, *and* knowing when to say when, the magic number seems to be seven hours of sleep or more. That's one of the ways Dr. Phillip Eichling, a weight loss and sleep specialist at the University of Arizona, helps patients optimize their health and weight. He said, "One of my treatments is to tell them they should move from six hours to seven hours of sleep."

That'll be one hundred sixty dollars, please.

But he's not alone. As neuroscientist Robert Stickgold says, "It could be that a good chunk of our epidemic of obesity is actually an epidemic of sleep deprivation."

Sleep Deprived and Proud of It

Is it hard for you to get the sleep you need, or am I the only one who struggles with this?

I wish I could say I was the perfect role model, a horizontal pillar of strength when it comes to getting to bed on time. Unfortunately that would make this a work of fiction. Just the other day my agent said to me over the phone, "Hey, thanks for emailing me those revisions—at 1:16 in the morning!"

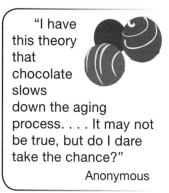

"I have this theory that chocolate slows down the aging process. . . . It may not be true, but do I dare take the chance?"

Anonymous

You and I are under a lot of pressure to stay busy and productive. So much that it may be tempting to buy into the Wonder Woman/Martyr Mom mentality that says, "Real Women Don't Need Sleep." I *really* hate to admit this, but sometimes I actually feel a little guilty about sleeping in, catching forty winks, or telling my kids to put themselves to bed because I'm turning in early.

If you feel the same way, don't.

Sleep is an amazing gift from our Creator. It's during sleep that our bodies heal and even our brains rebalance. When we sleep well we think more clearly, age slower, weigh less, avoid more disease, and live longer.

Even King David had something great to say about sleep when he wrote, "In vain you rise early and stay up late, toiling for food to eat—for [God] grants sleep to those he loves" (Ps. 127:2 NIV). The Amplified Bible says it this way: "He gives blessings to His beloved in sleep." David is talking about the futility of our efforts unless God is in charge of our lives. And yet the image he paints of sleep is a really great one.

I think I'll write his words on a nice card and keep it by my bed where I can see it nightly when I turn in. Maybe you'll want to do the same.

You're Feeling Sleepy, Very Sleepy

So what happens when we get to bed on time . . . but can't seem to fall asleep? What happens when sleep eludes us, leaving us to roll and twitch and study the numbers on the clock? You and I know that some nights we can't seem to fall asleep, no matter how hard we try. According to researchers and scientists, there are things we can do to improve our sleep habits and patterns:

Exercise regularly, but not in the last several hours before bed. Develop a habit of a relaxing nightly ritual like reading a book or listening to music. Use your bedroom for sleep or love—not as an office or gym—and it'll be easier to condition yourself to start to relax as soon as you walk into the room. Wear warm socks to bed because some folks say warm feet mean deeper sleep. Keep the temperature in your bedroom cool since cooler temperatures help our bodies prepare for sleep. Keep your room as dark as you can because even a small light—from a night-light or even your alarm clock—can cause your body to produce less melatonin, the hormone that tells your body how long and how deeply to sleep. Consider taking a synthetic melatonin supplement—you can find one online or at health stores and many markets—an hour before bed.

Don't drink a lot before bedtime to circumvent those midnight potty breaks. Avoid alcohol, caffeine, nicotine, and even late-night snacks. And if you can't fall asleep, don't just lay there. Turn on a light and read something boring (not this book, I hope!) until you're sleepy again.

Of course, if stress is keeping us awake, there are a couple ways to empty our heads of all those worrisome thoughts so the sandman can do his job. Sometimes I realize that actually writing that email or paying that bill would take less time than lying awake all night worrying about it—so I get out of bed, do the thing I'm dreading, then climb back between the sheets relieved and sleepy.

Sometimes it's not a single dreaded project but a hundred small loose ends that are keeping me awake. If that's the case, turning on the light, grabbing notebook and pen, and making a list of everything swimming through my head can eliminate that "What am I forgetting?" feeling and help me fall asleep.

Listening to music can distract my spinning brain long enough to fall asleep.

And of course, when it comes to the best recipe for rest, talking honestly to God and relinquishing my cares into his capable hands can't be beat.

This chapter may be a little different than the others. But there's no way to talk about the *real* cravings behind our food cravings without talking about slumber. So when it comes to the relationship between sleep and those unwanted pounds, four little words seem to say it all: you snooze, you lose.

Living the Sweet Life

- Take a look at your bedroom. How many functions does it serve? Do the exercise bike, TV, desk, and free weights *really* belong in your sleep-retreat/

love-nest? Maybe you can't remodel your bedroom overnight, but can you identify three things you can do today that will make your bedroom a more relaxing place to sleep tonight?

- What patterns have you noticed in your life? Do you crave more junk food or make more careless food choices when you're tired? Any thoughts on how you might prevent this from happening as often in the future?

- Do you have any weird feelings about bedtime that are sabotaging your shut-eye? After my divorce, bedtime meant time to lie still and panic, which is why I stopped going to bed altogether and got into the habit of staying busy until whatever time I dropped off to sleep out of sheer exhaustion. Every single night for about two years I fell asleep at my desk, at the kitchen table, on a couch, or on the floor, and one time while leaning on the dryer. (Do *not* try this at home! The habit I'm describing was performed by a professional basket case and should not be attempted by amateurs.) But back to you. How do *you* feel about bedtime? Are you avoiding your bed? If so, why? How can you begin to address the issues making you feel that way?

10

Clarity

About five years ago I got my bellybutton pierced.
You're probably thinking "Midlife Mom Goes Wild."
And of course you would be right. But it was still fun.
It didn't even hurt as much as I thought it would. I liked
everything about it, from the ring itself to the comfort-
zone-busting experience of getting pierced.

Okay, almost everything. The one exception was this
sign on the wall of the tattoo shop. It said, "Don't torture yourself. Let me do it instead." *That* was a little
disturbing.

I'm, like, *so* not into torture. Not even in movies. I can
handle anything else in a flick. Blood. Guts. Language.
Sex. Overwrought sentimentalism. And I love all genres.
Chick flicks. Romantic comedies. Action flicks. Psycholog-

ical thrillers. When it comes to movies, you name it and I can get happily lost in the celluloid images for hours.

I never saw *Braveheart* in the theater, but when it came out on video, my husband was first in line to rent a copy. When he brought it home, I caught a glimpse of ruggedly gorgeous Mel Gibson on the case and said, "Cool! This is supposed to be really good."

He said, "I hear there's lots of blood. You okay with that?"

"Bring it on! Anything but torture. Definitely no torture."

Now I know that the movie ends with a really graphic torture scene. But back then I was clueless, proceeding innocently into the flickering den with my Diet Coke in one hand and a bowl of popcorn in the other. Two hours later I found myself watching the scene through the cracks between my fingers, the image all squeezed and distorted, as if shrinking the viewing surface would shrink the impact.

Nah, it was still horrible.

I don't think I'm such an odd duck. I mean, who *likes* torture? Besides tattoo artists. The rest of us tend to avoid pain. Even when I got my belly button pierced, I asked for novocaine or Advil or at least a piece of ice for a little navel numbing before the big event. Of course, Dr. Sadistic merely threw back his head and howled maniacally before reaching for the pliers, but, hey, a girl's gotta try.

I'm probably doing all this thinking about pain and torture because of the kind of day I've had so far. I mean, it's really been agonizing.

The first thing that happened was that my laptop died. To make matters worse, it died with the first eighty-seven pages of this manuscript locked in its despicable bowels. Three weeks before deadline, no less. And please don't ask me if I have a backup disk. Three people have already asked me that question today, and I'm running out of places to hide the bodies. Paul Scalzo, computer wizard extraordinaire, is coming over in the morning to try to save me. If you opened this book and discovered that the page numbers began at eighty-eight, you'll know he failed.

Then there's the small matter of my deadbeat renters. See, the bank and I own this little rental house near Denver. Actually the bank owns pretty much all of it, but being good sports, they let me pay all the bills, deal with the tenants, collect the rent, and send it to them along with two hundred dollars of my own each month to cover the mortgage. By my calculations it's been a rewarding experience for my renters and my bank, not to mention my local pharmacist, who keeps me supplied with Excedrin and Tums. As for me, I've just been happy to help all these people out because—as a single mom raising two girls, one Boston terrier, and a little Cain now and then—sometimes I not only run out of bonbons, the afternoon sun glints off my big screen TV, obscuring my favorite soap opera and leaving me desperate for something to do. In any case, this situation is no longer working out well for me because said renters have decided to stop paying said rent while said bank has continued expecting said mortgage. So after my computer bailed on me, I spent the rest of the morning dealing with that little fiasco. And *that* was before I tried to activate the cell phone I bought on eBay for $140 and discovered it not only refuses to work, it seems to have no intention of working, having apparently applied for food stamps, disability, and welfare.

By midafternoon I was definitely in pain. Unlike *Braveheart's* William Wallace, I still had my intestines intact, but my sanity was definitely in shreds.

Pain-Free Living through Carbohydrates

The first time I gave birth, I was so convinced natural childbirth was the way to go, I told my doctor ahead of time I didn't want anything for the pain. Not even Advil. Not only did I believe a drug-free birth would give my baby a variety of health advantages, I actually embraced the pain as my initiation into a sisterhood of sorts. After all, from the dawn of time, women have undergone these very same agonizing labors of love to give life to generations of sons and daughters, and I considered it an honor to prepare myself to join their ranks.

The second time I gave birth, I begged for drugs.

"The chocoholics twelve-step program: Never be more than twelve steps away from chocolate."
Terry Moore

I admit it. I'm a wimp. Some people have high thresholds for pain, whether physical pain or emotional distress. Watching them sail through life is like watching an Olympic athlete pole vault over the crossbar with inches to spare.

My threshold for pain is kind of like tripping over Berber carpet. It's ridiculously low and it *still* sends me reeling.

So I have no qualms about admitting that, yes, when I'm in any kind of pain, I just want it to stop. And honestly, I don't see anything wrong with that. I guess what I have a problem with is *how* I make it stop.

How do I spell relief? I spell relief C-A-R-B-O-H-Y-D-R-A-T-E-S.

Of course, I wasn't consciously thinking any of this around four this afternoon when I got out an eight-by-eight-inch Pyrex baking dish, filled it with three pieces of cake with caramel icing, then added several scoops of vanilla ice cream. I don't think I was fully aware of my ulterior motives until the third bite, when my thoughts skipped ahead in anticipation of how I would feel ten minutes into the future when my plate was licked clean. I knew that by the time my empty dish was in the sink, I'd be feeling pretty lethargic and a lot less in touch with all the problems of my day. I might even feel a nap coming on. Chances are that broken computers, problem renters, and secondhand cell phones wouldn't seem nearly so catastrophic. With all that fat and sugar clogging my brain and body, I'd probably be thinking, why worry at all? Why not just deal with it all another day?

Unfortunately, by another day I'd be further behind on my manuscript, I'd have lost more rent, and—who knows?—my unscrupulous eBay seller might have changed his user ID and skipped town before refunding my money.

If You *Have* to Sacrifice Your Chocolate for Baking...

Assuming you haven't already eaten all the chocolate chips or baking bars in your kitchen, here are some helpful tips you can use the next time a recipe calls for melted chocolate:

- When you need to melt chocolate, begin by cutting or breaking chocolate into half-inch pieces or smaller. Nibbling it down to the right size works too.
- I don't care if you're in a hurry—high heat is not your friend. Chocolate burns easily, and you know how that tastes!
- The direct heat method for melting chocolate does not mean waving a candy bar over a candle flame. Instead, constantly stir chocolate pieces in a saucepan over low heat.
- Don't use direct heat for chocolate you plan to dip, mold, or scarf up from the pan.
- If you have a double boiler, that's nice. The rest of us just plop our chocolate in a metal mixing bowl and juggle it on top of a saucepan of hot but not boiling water.
- To melt chocolate in your microwave, begin by heating on medium for 1 to 1 1/2 minutes. Stir and reheat for another 30 seconds. Keep up this annoying process until only small lumps remain. You might be tempted to devour the seductively smooth sauce at this point, but take a deep breath and keep stirring until all the chocolate is melted. Then count to ten, grab a spoon, polish off the chocolate, and tell yourself that tomorrow is a better day for baking anyway.

In other words, by self-medi-caking, I could pretty much guarantee that not only would my pain over these problems be prolonged, my problems would end up multiplied as well. Somewhere between that third and fourth mouthful of cake, it dawned on me that if I wanted to put a permanent end to my discomfort, I needed to stop dulling my senses with junk food so I could think clearly enough to come up with some creative solutions.

All of a sudden my carb-addicted brain coughed up an image. It was a scene from the movie *Braveheart*. No, it wasn't the gruesome torture scene. It was a scene *before* the gruesome torture scene, when the woman in love with William Wallace visits him in his dungeon cell just hours before his execution by disembowelment. Desperate to help him, she hands him a vial of something.

"Drink this," she whispers. "It will dull your pain."

Wallace turns it down, saying, "It will numb my wits, and I must have them all."

Indeed, by staying clearheaded he bests his enemies and brings an end to his suffering, dying a swift and honorable death while managing in the process to inspire Scotland to victory against their oppressors.

Unlike William Wallace, I have problems that are neither epic nor noble. Nevertheless, I pondered his words as I stared down at the dish with the cake-and-ice-cream monstrosity still in my hands. All those carbs and sugars would *definitely* numb my wits, and to be honest, I was going to need every last one of those evasive little scamps if I wanted to solve the problems at hand.

Just When You Thought It Was Safe to Go Back in the Water

Gunky junk food isn't the only thing that can numb our wits. Sometimes the reason we can't think clearly is because our emotional and mental resources are needed elsewhere.

Remember the old rule "wait thirty minutes after eating before swimming"? This rule was based on the idea that when you swim, your muscles require extra blood flow and oxygen to keep you afloat. This is all well and good unless all that extra blood and oxygen has already been diverted to your stomach, which also needs extra blood and oxygen to digest lunch. Today the word on the street—or at the pool—is that our bodies have plenty of blood and oxygen to satisfy simultaneous digesting *and* casual swimming.

But regardless of how you manage your next postprandial swim, I think the underlying question is a helpful one: What do we do when limited resources are legitimately needed in two different places? I say this because sometimes the brain can feel thwarted— and our clear thinking compromised—because all our energies are being diverted to a different organ: our hearts.

Several months ago my mom and I were enjoying cups of hot chocolate at her house and talking about this topic when she said, "You know, the most helpful advice you ever gave me was on this subject, and it was during that time after Mother died."

I knew what she was referring to. One night about ten years ago my mom phoned me. I was living in Texas at the time, and she was in California and facing a hearth-wrenching situation. First thing next morning she was to meet the executor of her mom's estate—my grandmother had died eight months earlier of a heart attack—at the home in which her parents and grandparents had lived for more than sixty years. There she'd have a series of two-minute deadlines to make her selections from among the family heirlooms, photographs, and personal belongings her parents had left behind. It was an odd distribution process, to be sure. Everything in the house had been reorganized and shuffled into various "lots," and my mom had been given less than a day to study the list to figure out which lot might contain the ring her mother had promised her, the books her father had loved, or the heirloom china that had been passed down through generations of women and now belonged with her.

It was going to be an emotionally exhausting process any way you looked at it.

What made the entire event even more impossible was the fact that other than the executor, no one had been allowed in my grandmother's home in the eight months since she had died.

On the phone the night before all this was to occur, my mom said to me, "I know I need to stay objective in order to think clearly and get through the day. I also know the minute I walk through the front door my heart will pick up where it left off eight months ago, the day Mother died. Part of me still expects to walk in that house and hear her call out my name. I have so much grieving left to do, and it's going to hit me like a hurricane tomorrow morning. How in the world will I ever stay composed and keep my wits about me long enough to get through the day?"

Living thirteen hundred miles away, I knew that going with my mom to the house in the morning wasn't an option. Any strength I could offer had to come over the phone.

We talked for a long time and eventually I said, "You know, your heart has a right to grieve. Try this: Make a date with your heart. Starting tonight, talk to your grief. Say, 'In two weeks—say, on the fifth of next month at ten o'clock in the morning—you and I have an appointment. I promise that on that day we'll cry together and reminisce and wrestle with the horrible loss.' Say it again when you wake up. And when you walk into the house tomorrow morning and grief tugs hard at your sleeve, say it again. Throughout the day, keep reminding your grief to be patient. You and your heart definitely have work to do . . . but tomorrow's not the day. Tomorrow you've got to think clearly."

Reminiscing a decade later, my mom reminded me of that phone call and then added, "Those words got me through the day."

"I never thought to ask," I said, "did you have that date with your heart a couple weeks later, or was just the idea of it enough to get you through?"

"I kept that date. I spent the morning alone, writing in my journal. Later I went for a walk. I cried off and on. I needed that time to begin healing more deeply over the loss of my mom, and I was finally able to do it with undivided attention."

Can Two Wrongs Make Things Right?

Overeating can dull our wits. An overload of stress or grief can do the same thing. A third thing that can rob us of clarity is our own quick-fix choices.

When a friend of mine found out her husband had been frequenting dating sites and writing to various women, her initial response was to get back at him by having an affair of her own. She fantasized about it for several weeks. Eventually she crossed it off her list. Years later she told me why: "Having an affair would have made me bonkers just when I needed to think and act clearly. I was feeling betrayed—did I want to add guilt into the mix? We had decisions to make. Could our marriage be saved? Would my husband be faithful in the future? Could we trust each other again? I wanted truth. I knew if I made our lives messier, I'd be more prone to make a mistake. I could end up divorcing a repentant man because I'd gotten messed up with someone else. I could also end up staying with an unfaithful jerk because my affair had somehow 'balanced the scales' and now we felt even. I couldn't take either risk."

My friend and her husband are still together. Healthily. Happily. Faithfully. It's plain to see that this clearheaded woman made a wise choice.

I Can Think Clearly Now

I was thirteen when Johnny Nash topped the charts with "I Can See Clearly Now." You remember how the lyrics go, right? The rain is gone, the dark clouds that had kept him blind are gone, and suddenly he can see clearly all the obstacles in his way. Because of that, it's gonna be a bright, sunshiny day.

I loved this song back when my wardrobe consisted primarily of tube tops and bell-bottoms, and I love it still. I especially like the idea that bright, sunshiny days require not the absence of obstacles but only being able to see them *clearly*.

We will always have obstacles in our lives. When we can see and think clearly, we have a better chance of navigating our way safely around them. Back in chapter 3 I wrote about the importance of escape, and for good reason—there are definitely times when a little escapism is just what the doctor ordered. But not when there are problems to solve. In those moments, self-medi-caking is not the answer. Temporary relief might be spelled I-C-E C-R-E-A-M, but long-term solutions are wrought through clarity.

Several weeks have passed since I began writing this chapter. To bring you up to date, Paul was indeed able to save my computer (and my manuscript!). My renters have moved out, and with a little luck (not to mention a few coats of paint and a bulldozer), I'll have the house back on the market in a week or two. My cell phone has been replaced with one that works. Mel Gibson is just as ruggedly gorgeous as ever. I haven't even been tempted to reenact my Pyrex dish/sheet cake/ice cream debacle, *and* I hear they're having a two-for-one body piercing special at the tattoo parlor.

Clearly, life is good.

Living the Sweet Life

- How do you cope with pain?
- Can you think of a time you "numbed out" in a way that kept you from solving a problem at hand? How might you have handled things differently if you had kept your wits about you?
- Avoidance feels great—no one's disputing that fact! But the long-term complications don't feel good at all. Has procrastination or avoidance ever transformed a petite problem into a complicated crisis in your life?
- The next time you feel the urge to use food or sin to escape life's problems, what other choices can you make? What can you do to keep your wits about you so you can solve the problem at hand? Just as we stock our medicine cabinet with appropriate ways to manage pain, is there anything you can do today so that the next time you're hurting, you'll have resources on hand to help you manage the hurt wisely while you address the problem causing the pain?

11

Control

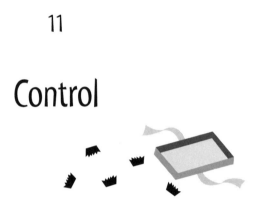

At the exact moment we passed the scraggly shrub that grows near the entrance to the freeway, Kacie looked at the dashboard clock and groaned, "We're gonna be late!"

Eternal optimist that I am, I chirped, "Not necessarily!"

Unfortunately, Kacie was right. We'd been making this drive nearly every morning now for several months, and it never failed. Whenever we got to that particular shrub before 7:30 a.m., she made it to school on time. After 7:30, she was *always* tardy.

The clock read 7:32.

I can vouch that Kacie is indeed my daughter. She is not a changeling brought home by mistake. And yet, unlike her eternally tardy mother, she hates being late. It drives her nuts, which would explain why, on this particular morning, she was close to tears.

"Kacie, cheer up. Maybe today we'll make it on time."

Actually, we'd done pretty well. When I'd made the spur-of-the-moment decision to move an hour south to Colorado Springs, I'd promised my fifth grader that I wouldn't ask her to switch schools in the middle of the year. As a result, four mornings a week Kacie and I had been driving forty-five minutes to Highlands Ranch so I could drop her off at school, take my laptop to a coffee shop, write for six hours, pick her up, and commute forty-five minutes back home. Since starting this crazy schedule, she had only been late a couple times, an odd contrast to the frequent tardies she got when we lived a mere eight minutes from her school. Go figure.

All that to say, I wasn't sure why she was so upset. Especially in light of the No-Fault-Tardy Cash Consolation Prize.

She must have remembered the prize at that very moment, because suddenly she said gloomily, "You owe me five bucks."

It was true. I won't bore you with details (timely kid, chronically late mom, use your imagination), but somehow we had initiated the policy of a five-dollar cash payment to Kacie whenever she was late to school. Another child might have tried to milk the system, hitting the snooze button a few times to pay for a new iPod. But Kacie merely continued her ongoing

A tasty sample from
The Chocolaphile Files

"My four-year-old daughter really influenced my decision to lose weight. I wanted to stay alive for her."

Michelle Willett

campaign to get me out the door on time.

I agreed with her that if she was indeed late, she would be the recipient of a fiver. But not even the possibility of money seemed to cheer her up. Ten minutes down the highway, she remained moody and morose.

"Look, Kacie, I don't mind paying you five bucks, but I'm not *that* lousy a businesswoman. I'm not giving away perfectly good money. I'm buying something with those dollars."

"Like what?"

"Like a good attitude and a smile."

"*What?*"

"That's right. If you accept the money, you're agreeing to my terms, and you have to cheer up. If you insist on staying grouchy, you forfeit the moolah."

"Fine, don't pay me then."

"You're kidding, right? You're going to give up five whole dollars so you can keep your bad mood?"

She seemed to consider my words carefully. Then she said, "Yep."

"Babe, let's think about this a minute. Unless you've got a time machine in that backpack of yours, whatever time you'll be arriving at school is no longer in your control. The window of opportunity when we might have gotten out of the house faster has come and gone. But there is something you *can* control right now, and it's whether you end the morning with five dollars in your pocket or not. *That* window of opportunity is open for about another ten minutes or so, and then it will have come and gone too. So whatcha gonna do?"

Sorry, Wrong Window

Remember when drive-ups consisted of *one* window? Granted, some still do, but increasingly I find myself pulling through fast food joints with two windows. At the first window someone takes my money. At the second window someone else gives me food. I haven't even mastered the two-window gig yet, and guess what I discovered near my house? A McDonald's with two lanes and *three* windows. I'm all for options, but this is ridiculous. More times than not, I accidentally pass the first window and try to pay at the second, or brake at the first window only to realize no one's there and I'm supposed to drive forward after all.

Seems like I'm always waiting at the wrong window.

And I'm not just talking fast food. Unfortunately, I find myself idling vainly in front of closed windows of opportunity as well. No wonder I'm often frustrated to the point of chocolate!

I'm really freaking out, for example, over the forty-five pounds I've put on (yes, I know it was thirty-five pounds at the beginning of this book, but what's a deadline without chocolate?). I can't change the fact that I've done that. I also can't change hurts from my past. Or the price of tea in China. Or the fact that when I bought this house, I didn't get the lowest interest rate because I'd been late on a handful of credit card payments. Ouch.

The windows of opportunity in which I might have kept these things from occurring have long since slammed shut. So why do I keep parking there, idling my engine, staring at my reflection in the empty panes and wishing for chances gone by?

Not too long ago I heard my engine idling again and smelled all those noxious exhaust fumes building up, and a lightbulb went off in my brain. Here's what I realized: While I'm busy lamenting a few things I long to control and can't, my life is filled with literally hundreds of things I *can* control and don't.

This means that while I can't undo hurts from the past, here's what I *can* do: I can take charge of my life *today*, refusing to give those memories any authority in my life over the next twenty-four hours, thinking instead about my blessings and successes, and practicing the kind of boundaries that might protect me from similar hurts in the future.

I can't change the fact that I couldn't fit into my cute jeans this morning, but here's what I *can* do: I can fix myself a healthy breakfast, stock my fridge with cherry tomatoes and baby carrots, and say yes when Kacie begs me to walk to the park with her.

I can't lower my interest rate today, but here's what I *can* do: I can open all my mail and make sure any bill that crosses my path today gets paid on time.

Just Do It Already

Sometimes I see my kids following in my wheel ruts and idling in front of closed windows. Like Kacie hanging onto the tardy bell blues. The good news is that when I pointed out what she was doing, she stopped lamenting the thing she could no longer control and embraced the thing she could still control. I have to give her credit for that. Heaven knows I've already given her enough cash.

Kaitlyn too. For a while now she's been complaining about the five pounds she wants to lose. Now, you have to understand, she's not only nineteen, she's got this svelt/long-waisted/perky-figure/apricot-skin/gorgeous body thing going on. So for months whenever I've heard her bring up these five imaginary pounds, I've done what any sympathetic, supportive mother would do, which is jab my finger toward my tonsils, make gagging noises, and say, "Oh, puleeeeeeeeese." But recently it dawned on me that, while there's nothing wrong with wanting Kaitlyn to recognize her blessings, I also want her to know that she's in charge.

So the last time she brought this up, I put away my finger and said, "You have an amazing figure. But if you want to lose five pounds, do it. Otherwise, accept your beautiful body and stop whining. The thing I *don't* want you to do is get used to the feeling of spending months or years obsessing about something you can change without taking charge of your life and doing it."

Look, this isn't a new idea. We've all heard the simple prayer, "Lord, grant me the serenity to accept the things

I cannot change, the courage to change the things I can, and the wisdom to know the difference."

But sometimes hearing it and putting it into practice can be two different things.

What's on My Plate *Today?*

Sometimes the thing we long to control is not something that's already occurred but something that hasn't even happened yet. My friend Belinda Bai quotes a Chinese proverb that says, "Don't borrow sorrow from tomorrow." And yet that's exactly what we do.

Recently Kaitlyn, Kacie, and I were talking about this very thing. Their dad is dating a very nice woman. As for me, in the four years I've been separated and divorced, I haven't dated much, but naturally I think about it. As you can imagine, these can seem like scary, threatening developments to my daughters. They long to control their futures. Kacie asks, "What if I don't like a new stepmom or stepdad?" Kaitlyn says, "I can't stand the thought of someone new coming into our family."

Last night I confessed to both of them, "Sometimes when I think about the future, I have fears too. For example, I think about my parents dying, and I can't bear the thought. I know it will happen one day, but I have no idea how I will handle it. It's too painful to even consider. Then I remind myself, *Thank God that's not on my plate today. When it is on my plate, I trust that God will give me the resources I need to handle it.* Until then all I need to know is that it's not on my plate today. I know you have fears too, and you wonder how you'll handle certain things. But guess what? Those things are not on your plate today. And when they are, God will give you the resources you need to handle them."

I've really been trying to get a handle on this control thing. I mean, if you and I long for control, why in the world don't we cowboy up and do the things that will give us the control we seek?

What would happen if we stopped spending unnecessary hours idling our engines and wringing our hands in front of windows that are no longer open for business?

What would happen if we stopped lamenting the fifty things we *can't* control and focused our attention on the fifty *thousand* things we *can* control?

What would happen if we stopped whining about things we have the power to change and finally took charge of our lives and changed them?

What would happen if we stopped borrowing sorrow from tomorrow? If we got in the habit of asking ourselves, "What's on my plate *today?*"

You and I have *got* to learn how to embrace the control we seek. Because when we don't—when we long for control but don't get proactive and take charge of our lives—things can get ugly fast.

Objects in Mirror May Be Larger Than They Appear

I mentioned earlier that I haven't dated much. But last summer I did put my big toe in the water, seeing someone for a couple months. It was exciting and scary at the same time. I went from thinking we were a perfect match to wondering if it was the right timing to realizing this was a wonderful person but the wrong choice for me. The relationship ended, but I felt like it had been a close call. It was my pilot episode of *The New Dating Game* and I had yet to get a handle on the genre of the show: Sitcom? Psychological drama? Tragedy?

Shortly after that I began putting on a few pounds, then a few more. My upward climb was slow but steady. Why couldn't I seem to stop eating? Was I eating in response to stress? Perhaps I'd developed some weird nutritional deficit that made me crave trace minerals found in Twix bars and Ho Hos. I even wondered if I was responding to some primal seasonal instinct and bulking up for winter like a woodchuck or bear. To make matters even worse, during a church fundraiser I bought six tubs of frozen cookie dough. My plan was to give them away as Christmas presents, which, as you can imagine, explains at least two of my newfound dress sizes.

Several months later Kaitlyn heard about a new hair salon in town and bought us both gift certificates. How fun would *this* be! Besides, I desperately needed a good antidote for the frumps. I donned the chubby woman's fashion friend—black from head to toe—and drove to meet Kaitlyn.

Walking into the salon, we were greeted by the aroma of incense and the strains of international music. Salon owners Enrique and Venus welcomed us warmly, then Venus handed us two clipboards and said, "Before we start, please take a seat and fill out these questionnaires. Enrique and I practice the art of hair feng shui, and your answers to this questionnaire will help us craft a hairstyle in harmony with your personal energies."

I scanned the clipboard before reading the first question aloud: "What color represents your truest self during even-numbered months, winter solstice notwithstanding: red, yellow, blue, purple, teal, sea foam green, or beige?"

Venus gave a dismissive little wave. "Don't spend a lot of time thinking about your answers. Just read the question, immediately close your eyes, and write down whatever color you see."

She left and Kaitlyn whispered, "Is 'eyelid' a color?"

I said evenly, "Cynicism is not an attractive color on you. I always thought of you as more of a winter. Just close your eyes and answer the question, will you?"

When we finished, Kaitlyn met with Venus and I met with Enrique for our personal feng shui hair consultations.

Enrique offered me bottled water, then took a few minutes to peruse my questionnaire. He nodded confidently before speaking. "I can see from your answers that you are earth-fire. I want your new hairstyle to both reflect and express your earth-fire nature. The hairstyle we choose also needs to reconcile struggles from your past with your desires for your future." He tapped the clipboard gently. "I noticed that here on question number twenty-three— *Have you experienced any recent changes in your body, looks, or personal style?*—you wrote that you'd recently put on some weight. Can you tell me why?"

It's unnerving when someone you've known all of two minutes asks you an intimately personal question and you blurt out an answer you didn't even know you had, but as soon as it leaves your lips you know deep in your heart it's true.

I didn't think about my answer at all. In fact, I don't remember thinking about anything, and I *definitely* wasn't thinking about relationship issues or dating or men, even though—as it turned out—these were the very things prompting my unexpected answer.

I simply shrugged and said, "I wanted out of the game," like I'd known it all along.

And maybe I had.

You're Not the Boss of Me

I'm not exactly the first woman in the course of history to use eating and weight to establish a boundary or gain an element of control in her life.

One woman interviewed for this book had this to say: "I've been praying about my eating habits lately because basically, if I want something, I eat it. I know I'm eating out of rebellion because my husband and kids can be extremely demanding. My husband may say, 'You shouldn't eat that,' and I think, 'So what?' I crave freedom to do what I want to do. I want some space. I don't want anybody to tell me what to eat or what not to eat. As a wife and mom, I sacrifice a lot, so when I find something to eat, by golly, I'm going to eat whatever I want."

Another friend of mine confessed that emotional eating was her way of saying, "Ha! My husband may control everything else in my life, but he can't control what I put into my body! I control that!"

One of my best friends from high school *doesn't* eat for the same reason. By controlling her body to the point of anorexia, she feels like she has a better grip on her chaotic world.

My marriage had been broken a very long time before it ended. At one point I put on a hundred unwanted pounds so I wouldn't feel vulnerable to affairs. It worked, but were my strategies really the best choices? Hey, I could be out in left field here, but I gotta wonder: The *next* time I don't want a relationship, what would happen if I just said *no*?

I'm still figuring out how to create boundaries and take control of my world in ways that don't make me huge, putting me in the same category as those frogs that swell up to four times their normal size when frightened. One wildlife website I checked said these frogs may also sway around in a threatening and fierce manner and emit a foul odor. I don't want to do that either.

We don't have to put a lot of thought into longing for control. Whether we're ten years old or a hundred and ten, it just sort of happens. But embracing the healthiest ways to *get* that control is a different matter altogether. *That* takes intentional thought. And wisdom. And planning. And deliberate action. And whenever you can arrange it, that cash consolation prize is *never* a bad idea.

Living the Sweet Life

- Are you using food or weight to make your life feel safer or to control things or even relationships in your life?

- You know the serenity prayer that says, "Lord, grant me the serenity to accept the things I cannot change, the courage to change the things I can, and the wisdom to know the difference"? Get a piece of notebook paper and write that prayer one hundred times. Just kidding. Instead, think of one thing that is within your power to change and make up your mind to change it. Ask God for insight and a game plan. Then tell one person what you're going to change and how you're going to start.

- Are you parked in front of certain windows, idling your engine, longing for the chance to go back in time? If you really can't do anything about a lost opportunity, ask God to help you let go and move on. If need be, ask a friend to pray with you. Begin today to thank God for helping you let go.

12

Transformation

Do you ever feel like a caterpillar?

Caterpillars eat pretty much nonstop. The caterpillar of the Polyphemus moth is the hungriest, eating up to 86,000 times its own weight. This can be compared to a baby eating 273 tons of food. Or a grown woman pigging out on—don't laugh, I did the math—60 million, 200 thousand Quarter Pounders.

I've yet to stumble across research linking the voracious appetite of the Polyphemus caterpillar to emotional eating, but what else could it be? I mean, there she is, stuck in a rut, inching along when what she'd *really* love to do is shed her baggage and learn to fly. Is it any wonder she drowns her sorrows in Norway maple leaves and milkweed?

Caterpillars aren't the only creatures that binge eat even as they long for transformation. I've been there, haven't you? Sometimes we crave change because we're bored. Or hurting. Or just plain frustrated. Sometimes the milkweed looks greener on the other side of the fence. Sometimes the transformation we crave is not into someone we have yet to become but into someone we were back before time and circumstances took their toll.

Several years ago I was cruising a high school reunion website when I felt my heart lurch to a standstill and the room begin to spin.

Ohmigosh. There it was. *His* name.

Talk about transformation! Never mind the jar of estrogen cream sitting on my bathroom counter at that very moment. Suddenly I was fifteen again and in love for the very first time. I had Farrah Fawcett hair. I smelled like Jean Nate and Clearasil. If I had looked in a mirror right then, I probably would have been wearing a peasant blouse and my favorite blue jean skirt, the one I'd made by ripping out the leg seams of my hip-huggers and filling in the gaps with triangles of paisley fabric.

Mark was twenty-one and had worked in my dad's print shop since high school, evolving into my dad's right-hand man. My parents suspected we were sweet on each other—what they didn't know was that we had been secretly seeing each other for nine months, falling madly in love.

I remember the morning I snuck out of the house early to meet Mark before school, just like we always did. We kissed and talked about the wedding, house, and babies we wanted. Mark said we should tell my parents we were in love; I said it was too soon. Five hours later at my house, our little world crashed and burned. I'll spare you the gory details, but suffice it to say that my folks had discovered evidence of our star-crossed romance (can you say *diary*?). After considerable drama, they banished me to my room and Mark from our lives.

I never saw or heard from him again.

Twenty-seven years later I found myself staring at his name on my computer screen. Imagine! After nearly three decades, contact was only a few keystrokes away!

Here We Go Again

You know where this is headed, don't you?

My first email was of the "Do you remember me . . ." variety. I checked my inbox a dozen times a day for a week before Mark answered. I had feared the worst, but he'd simply been on vacation. He was as happy to hear from me as I'd been to find him.

In no time at all, we caught up on spouses and children and careers—I learned Mark lived three states away and was married with two children and a successful legal career; he learned I was recently separated and had children and a career of my own. As you can imagine, it didn't take long for us to leave the "safe" territory of statistics and resumes and venture into the minefield of memories that had been waiting nearly three decades to be disarmed.

We had so many questions for each other! I learned that following the blowup at my house, Mark sought out my dad at the print shop, begging him not to blame me. Mark pleaded, "It was all my fault; forgive her." He also spent several hours in the office of my pastor, telling him what had happened and asking him to make sure my family was all right. Mark also told me that after losing me he did little but sleep and grieve, and that it was a year before he began to date again.

We both confessed to trying to locate each other through the years. I'd called directory assistance on several occasions; he'd used the computer at the sheriff's department where he'd been a deputy before passing the bar exam.

Eventually we exchanged phone numbers. The moment I picked up the phone and heard his voice, the decades melted away. The years had lent more gravel to his voice, but it was still him, the man I'd once loved with the kind of insane, untried devotion only a fifteen-year-old can muster.

Once loved?

Ha! Who was I kidding? Looked to me like I was falling for him all over again.

From Dr. Jekyll to Mr. Hyde?

Even friends and family noticed the difference. Linda said, "You're all glowy!" Michelle said, "Wow, you seem happy lately!" My mom sighed and said, "You're up to something, aren't you?"

What a mess. I'd been transformed, all right, but not necessarily for the better.

One day on the phone I blurted, "Mark, this is *so* wrong. You're married, and I *don't* want to fall in love with you again, and I *don't* want to be 'the other woman' in your life! We need to stop calling each other."

He reluctantly agreed. I cried as I hung up the phone, but I also felt relieved. I knew it was the right thing to do.

Every day was such a struggle! To keep from picking up the phone, I scheduled every waking moment with meetings or with family or friends. I told my mother, sisters, and best friend what was happening in my life. I also booked several sessions with a Christian counselor, hoping that together we could diffuse some of my feelings. When it came to getting over Mark, I'd gone "cold turkey." I kept hoping that our total "fast" from each other would get easier. Unfortunately, each day seemed more difficult than the last!

After two weeks I called him. He was as relieved to hear my voice as I was to hear his. Our daily conversations resumed. Some days I took the high road, insisting we were going to "do the right thing" and stay out of trouble. Other days I joined him in making plans to rendezvous halfway between his state and mine.

On two more occasions I put a stop to our phone conversations. I figured that from an emotional and spiritual standpoint, we were already involved in an affair. Still, I was certain that through accountability and my own personal grit and determination to "do the right thing," I could avoid falling deeper into trouble. Some days I literally shouted through my teeth, "I *won't*

give in to temptation! I *won't* give in to temptation!"
Unfortunately, despite my best teeth-clenching efforts,
Mark and I couldn't seem to stay away from each other.
We had yet to meet in person, but I knew it was just a
matter of time.

I'd been transformed from midlife mom to lovesick
chick. I was also teetering on the brink of full-scale
adultery. It was dawning on me that maybe some trans-
formations aren't all that prudent. I couldn't help but
think of the wizard's duel in *The Sword in the Stone*.
In the Disney movie based on T. H. White's classic
story, Merlin transforms himself into a mouse just as
his nemesis transforms herself into a cat. *Oops*. I'd
been transformed too, but it wasn't working out any
better for me than it had for Merlin. Like the leg-
endary wizard, I needed to scramble fast for another
change.

The transformation I sought this time around seemed
daunting: I needed desperately to change my heart.
That's hard to do under normal circumstances but pretty
near impossible when you no longer own the deed to
your own heart because you've given it clean away to
someone else.

Surrender

I'd done everything I could think of doing to stay out
of trouble. I figured it was time to call in the cavalry.
Or call on Calvary.

That's exactly what I did. I called out to God. Except
it was kind of a weird prayer. I didn't pray for strength.

Instead I admitted defeat, asked for rescue, and begged for transformation.

My prayer went like this: "Lord, you know my heart. I'm doing my best here, but the truth of the matter is that left on my own, I'm going to end up in bed with this man. Call it anything you want—sin nature, unfinished business, lust, midlife crisis—but it's stronger than I am and I can't fight it anymore. So I'm giving up. I'm asking you to do the battle for me. Change my heart, Lord. It's beyond me to do it. It's going to have to be you."

I wish I could say that the next day my behavior completely changed. It didn't. When I could stay busy and off the phone with Mark, I did just that. When I couldn't, I refused to beat myself up about it. I just thanked Jesus for forgiving me for my failings and continued asking him to do battle for me.

Within a week, my prayers began to change. I continued asking the Holy Spirit to "do the right thing" through me, but I took it one step further. I asked him to put into my heart the kinds of desires he wanted me to have. As the words left my mouth, I realized what an amazing request this was. Eight days earlier, I couldn't have yielded my heart in this fashion—after all, if I had asked the Lord to help me to hunger for godly things, wouldn't that mean my desire for Mark would have to go? So when the words came naturally, I realized that God was doing exactly what I had asked him to do: He was fighting this battle for me! His Spirit, in me, was enabling me to pray for things I never could have asked for on my own!

Keep Me Searching for a Heart of Gold

A few nights later I found myself home alone for the evening. I fidgeted restlessly, my eyes darting to the phone every few minutes. I knew Mark was working late at the office that night, and I wanted to call him so badly I could taste it.

I WILL be strong. I WILL be strong. I WILL be strong.

I eyed the handset, rehearsing his number in my head.

You can do this. Be strong. Resist the devil and he will flee from you.

I chewed my bottom lip and inched closer to the phone.

And then I had a thought. It went something like this: "You're lonely and you'd like some companionship. Fine. So why does it need to be Mark? You want to spend the evening with someone? Spend it with Jesus."

I turned on a CD of praise and worship music, lit a few candles, and turned down the lights. I snuggled into the couch. Over the next two hours, I sang. I also talked, and for once my prayers weren't a litany of my annoying problems and concerns. Instead I told the Lord all the things I appreciated about him and how grateful I was for his presence in my life! Sometimes I laughed out loud. Sometimes I sat quietly, let my thoughts rest, and simply listened.

At one moment I was sitting with my eyes closed, basking in his presence, when a beautiful picture came to mind. I imagined myself standing before the throne of God, letting his presence warm me like golden rays. As the light of his presence fell on my roughly hewn heart, my heart began to glow and then to change. Once primitive and rustic—little more than a clod of dirt, really—my heart began to take on the smooth lines and amber hues of polished gold.

I opened my eyes. I was still in my living room, the CD player still humming, the candle flames dancing on pools of melted wax. At first glance, everything was the same . . . and yet I realized nothing in my life would ever be quite the same. I broke into a huge smile. So *this* was the missing piece of the puzzle! Here, finally, was the secret to changing my clay heart into something finer!

We all know the story of King Midas, the fairy tale royal who bargained for the ability to turn everyday items into gold. A thousand years ago, medieval alchemists tried to turn fantasy into reality, spending entire lifetimes in search of a formula that could transform common things—mud and wood and lead—into gold. Even Sir Isaac Newton thought this kind of miracle was possible and, when he wasn't making applesauce, joined the quest for the knowledge that would produce this kind of transformation.

Today we shake our heads and wonder what the heck they were thinking! And yet, honestly, hadn't I been trying to do the exact same thing? I'd spent months treating my dirt-clod heart with my homemade elixir of grit and accountability. Unfortunately, while grit and accountability can certainly change behavior, they can't transform a clay heart into gold. For that kind of miracle, I didn't need a formula.

I needed God.

Getting to the Heart of the Matter

In the following days, I continued doing my best to stay off the phone with Mark and thanking God for forgiving me when I failed. I continued asking the Holy Spirit to fight this battle for me and to tuck his desires into my heart. Most importantly, I began to spend more and more time basking my heart in the glow of his presence. I was convinced as never before that by merely enjoying his presence, I could see my heart transformed in a way that all of my teeth-clenching determination could not accomplish!

My conversations with Mark dwindled from every day to every three or four days. Our topics of conversation changed too. Suddenly I was saying things like, "I don't want to have an affair! I don't want the heart wounds an affair would bring into my life and yours as well, and I don't want that kind of sin hindering my relationship with the Lord!"

Sure, I'd been saying those kinds of things all along, but for months the words had come from my head, chiseled with tremendous effort from the body of knowledge I'd accumulated over years of Sunday school, sermons, and personal study. Suddenly I was surprised to find the words flowing effortlessly from my heart, carried easily as though borne on a great river.

One day we simply stopped calling each other. It was the weirdest thing. There wasn't a single tear. We never actually even said good-bye.

I looked at the calendar.

It was almost three weeks from the night I'd sat with God in my candlelit living room and watched him begin the magic of taking one very muddy heart and transforming it into something new.

From Muddy Caterpillar to Golden Butterfly

To this day I still smile when I think of the whole thing. I still can't believe how difficult it was to transform myself—and how easy it became once I began sunning my muddy heart in the glow of the transforming presence of a holy God.

When it comes to making positive changes in my life, are accountability, determination, and counseling still in my arsenal of resources? You bet they are! But perhaps I've relied too much on personal grit and not enough on my powerful God.

But enough about me. Let's talk about you!

At the risk of mixing my metaphors, I've got a few questions for you: Have you ever been stuck in a rut, inching along, longing to be changed into something finer? Has your dirt-clod heart ever yearned to sprout wings and fly? Are you tired of pigging out on Norway maple and milkweed? Perhaps, instead of looking in the mirror and seeing the impact of every one of those 60,200,000 Quarter Pounders, you're ready to see something new. Something precious. Something beautiful.

Are you craving transformation?

I don't know the condition of your heart or what kind of transformation you might be longing for. I do know that the Bible has lots to say about the condition of your heart and mine. Here are some phrases that have been used to describe various conditions of the human heart:

- stubborn (Ps. 81:12)
- capable of going astray (Ps. 95:10)
- proud (Ps. 101:5)
- blighted and withered (Ps. 102:4)
- wounded (Ps. 109:22)
- filled with madness (Eccles. 9:3)
- afflicted (Isa. 1:5)
- faltering and trembling with fear (Isa. 21:4)
- harboring deceit (Prov. 26:24)
- far from God (Matt. 15:8)
- weighed down with anxieties (Luke 21:34)

If you've been longing for a change of heart, consider letting the Master Alchemist orchestrate your transformation from muddy caterpillar to golden butterfly. I know he can do it for you because he did it for me. He also did it for King David, who wrote, "When I called, you answered me; you made me bold and stouthearted" (Ps. 138:3 NIV). He also did it for the Israelites, promising them: "I will give you a new heart. . . . I will remove from you your heart of stone and give you a heart of flesh" (Jer. 36:26 NIV).

How can you begin letting God transform your heart? I really believe one way is by sunning your little dirt-clod caterpillar of a heart in his holy presence through praise and worship. I also believe in the power of surrender, asking the Holy Spirit for rescue and transformation.

And as you're thinking about all this, take a look at these heart-related verses. I love them because they remind me of the night I spent singing and resting in God's presence and the image I had of myself before the throne of God, letting my heart bask in the light of who he is!

> Trust in the Lord with all your heart and lean not on your own understanding.
>
> Proverbs 3:5 NIV

> Sing and make music in your heart to the Lord.
>
> Ephesians 5:19 NIV

> Set your hearts on things above, where Christ is seated at the right hand of God.
>
> Colossians 3:1 NIV

> For God . . . made his light shine in our hearts.
>
> 2 Corinthians 4:6 NIV

> This then is how we know that we belong to the truth, and how we set our hearts at rest in his presence.
>
> 1 John 3:19 NIV

The Polyphemus moth aside, sometimes transformation is not a job for do-it-yourselfers. Sometimes it's a job for deity. And who knows? Maybe as we embrace the changes he offers, we'll find ourselves a little less inclined to bury our sorrows in Milk Duds and Twinkies. Don't laugh. It's possible. After all, have you ever seen a chubby butterfly?

Living the Sweet Life

- Do you long for transformation? Tell me about it.
- How are you with the whole accountability thing? Can other people really hold you to making wiser choices when it comes to food or relationships or whatever? Does it make a difference whether their input is unsolicited or you've asked for their help? What qualities would you look for in a person you'd be willing to ask for this kind of help?
- When was the last time you spent time with God without asking him for anything? For a long time I could never figure out the attraction of praise and worship. A couple years ago I finally asked God to show me what worship could really be like, and he did. Does that sound like something you'd like to ask him to do for you?

A Little Something for Dessert

The Chocolaphile Files

We all crave something besides food, and it's cama-raderie. It's knowing that whatever we're struggling with, we're not "out there" all alone and abandoned. We want to be reminded that our problem is common and that other women not only relate, sometimes they can even come to our aid with insights and advice. And every now and then what we *really* want to know is that whatever stupid thing we've done, other people have done something stupider.

I get tons of emails from women who read my books. Here's one of my favorites, from a woman named Susan: "You've made me feel so much better about myself! I ran over my husband's cell phone charger with my minivan, but after reading your story I was able to brag that at least I hadn't run over his laptop computer! Thanks for lightening my heart."

See what I mean?

As I was working on this book, I asked friend and fellow author Beth Leuders to give me a hand by writing the sidebars you've been enjoying throughout this book. I also asked her to interview women about their chocolate addictions, emotional eating pitfalls, and strategies for survival. My plan was to use the information she gleaned just for research and background. But as I was reading the transcripts I found myself so encouraged and inspired that I knew these women deserved to have their own voices heard.

You've read snippets of their thoughts in earlier chapters, but here you'll find full-scale confessions, insights, survival tips, revelations, encouragement, and a few surprises to boot. For example, you're about to learn about the link between peppermint patties and frozen naked fantasies; how one ER nurse helps suicidal patients beef up their will to live; ideas for making your kitchen a safer place; how to uninvite yourself to your own pity party; why jiggling isn't *always* something to avoid . . . and much more!

So welcome to the Chocolaphile Files, where women who love chocolate share their recipes for coping and hoping and living a little better life. I hope you'll find yourself as entertained and inspired as I was!

"Stressed" Is "Desserts" Spelled Backwards

When I'm really stressed, I crave peppermint patties. Oh my gosh, I can just put one in my mouth and let it melt and be totally in heaven. My whole family is just as bad. If there's a death in the family, we'll all go out and get some chocolate. Or we'll sit together with our coffee and chocolate and take in everything together. My mother-in-law loves chocolate-covered chocolates. When my sister-in-law had surgery, I sent her M&M's. Everyone needs a little chocolate, especially women going through surgery.

There are days I dig through everything in the house because I've got to have my coffee and my chocolate. I'm talking chocolate cookies, chocolate icing in the refrigerator, old Halloween candy. I've even gone for the baking cocoa. But peppermint patties are my favorite. I think of those commercials where people take one bite of a York Peppermint Patty and suddenly they're imagining themselves skiing down a mountain. When I bite into a peppermint patty, I imagine myself wearing nothing but a coyote fur coat in the middle of Antarctica with my husband. How sexy is that?

Donna Perot, special education paraeducator

Put Your Reeboks Where Your Mouth Is

One of the guys at work had a jar of mini Snickers. You pop one of those in your mouth and all of a sudden you have twenty little wrappers in front of you.

I think I eat more out of boredom than out of a need for comfort. I get lazy too and go for foods that are fast and easy.

One of my daughters recently lost one hundred pounds. She did it by exercising more. She was a foreign exchange student in Ecuador and didn't have transportation, so she had to walk everywhere. She lost about forty pounds before she went, forty while she was gone, and another twenty to forty when she came back. Now she watches what she eats and makes an intentional effort to exercise.

I'm one of those people who loves to exercise to get the endorphins going. If I don't exercise, I get down. Sometimes when I'm stressed, instead of grabbing that candy bar, I'll opt for a walk. It feels great to get outside and grab a breath of fresh air, even if it's only a walk around the block.

Cathy Schwartz, accountant

Emotional Eating Survival Strategies

I've been through heavy-duty stress this past year. We've had deaths, heart attacks—not to mention three teenagers! Emotional eating is a major issue. Here are some things I've learned:

Get out of the habit of eating and watching television.

Make your home a safe place. Keep your kitchen safe from tempting foods. Just don't buy the junk stuff. I'm on medication that makes me crave carbohydrates—bread and cakes—so I don't keep tempting things in the house.

Stress smart. If I'm going to stress out, I like a cup of hot tea and toast with jelly.

Get support and tools. I joined Weight Watchers three years ago, and they have a chocolate-flavored protein smoothie. I mix that with milk and yogurt and have that every day. With this daily drink I don't even buy chocolate much anymore.

Don't deny yourself. If you like candy, have candy. If you like chocolate, have chocolate. The thing is to learn not to have lots of it every day. If I do get into one of those moods, I'll have a few bites and then throw the rest away.

Know God. My walk with the Lord and my prayer life really do make a big difference in my eating. I even ask God to show me foods that are safe to eat. It's easy to eat everything and anything when life feels like it's falling apart. Whether it's just everyday stress or a major crisis, I just about live on my knees.

Linda Hansen, Premier Design jewelry consultant

Typing Test, Drug Test, Chocolate Test ...

When I was CEO of a rehab company, everyone in my office knew CEO really stood for Chocolate Eating Officer. My CFO (Chief Financial Officer) was the Chocolate Finding Officer and I had a CAO (Chief Administration Officer) who doubled as the Chocolate Acquisitions Officer.

One year on my birthday I was walking into the building from the parking garage when I started seeing mini chocolate candy bars on the ground. I thought, "Who is spilling this stuff?" Picking up candy bars as I went, I got into our beautiful reception area and realized the candy bars led down the hall to my office.

I got there, and my office was covered. Desk, table, four chairs, credenza, bookshelf—every square inch was hidden by a chocolate bar. My employees even hung chocolate mobiles from the ceiling. I had to sweep my arm across my desk to clear a swath so I could work. Later that day I had an interview in my office. By then I'd adapted to the chocolate being everywhere. So I was sitting there interviewing this woman for a potential job with us, not even thinking about the chocolate. At one point she was saying something and her arm knocked against this big chocolate thing hanging from the ceiling. She was so totally unentertained by the whole thing that I knew right then she wouldn't get the job. If she didn't have a sense of humor, she'd have a hard time working with my company.

Months later I was still finding birthday chocolate in my office.

Karen DeLorenzo, executive management

Tell It Like It Is

Sometimes if I feel I've failed or made a mistake, I throw myself a pity party—with plenty of snacks! I think, "It doesn't matter if I get big and fat. It doesn't matter if I eat this anyway. I don't care."

Because I do love God, I feel like he's sitting there saying, "You don't need to be doing this." That motivates me to think differently. I tell myself, "God gave me everything in my life. He cares and so do I. I'm not going to have this pity party."

Then I usually look at what I thought was a failure and realize it wasn't that bad. I remind myself I'm okay and I don't need that snack. I start building myself back up. I do the positive self-talk thing. I say, "I work darn hard, and I'm good at what I do, and I didn't make that big a mistake. I am a good mom." I figure when it comes to what we tell ourselves, we can be our own worst enemy or our own best friend.

Donna Perot, special education paraeducator

Blackened Grilled Fish: No Pain *and* No Gain

When I get those insane chocolate cravings, my staples are gum, Velamints, and diet soda. I order sugar-free chocolate Velamints online. I also chew sugar-free Double Bubble gum, which I buy (in bulk!) from Wal-Mart. Sometimes diet chocolate soda, diet cream soda, or diet Sunkist can get rid of my sugar tooth.

For mealtimes, the George Foreman grill can't be beat. I start with frozen fish, add some blackening seasoning, and I've got grilled fish six minutes later. I use this grill every day and it's fabulous. Also, I'll never have to worry about getting fat on grilled fish! This has really helped get me feeling like I'm eating healthy without suffering!

Michelle Willett, police dispatcher

Chocolate: The Cure for Everything

Funny you should call right now. I was just eating these gourmet chocolates with these great names. One is titled "Tranquility." It's made of milk chocolate and lavender. "Renew" is dark chocolate with black currant, and "Rejoice" is milk chocolate with orange and crisp rice. "Forgiveness" is dark chocolate with lemon. These are made by a company called New Tree.

Of course, there are other benefits of chocolate too. Like fellowship. Chocolate is for celebration. They have this awesome chocolate shop in Orlando where you can have chocolate parties. You spend so much per person and you make chocolates and they have a chocolate fountain. It's a blast!

Another benefit has to do with nutrition. In a chocolate bar you have all the food groups you'll ever need. You've got milk for dairy, cocoa beans for vegetables, nuts for protein, and the crunchy part for breads.

Karen DeLorenzo, executive management

It Jiggles, but You Won't

Emotional eating is really bad, and yet we all do it. Why do women do this? Men don't seem to struggle like we do.

During the day I can be 100 percent faithful in eating, but anything after 8:00 at night, forget it—it's my buffet-o-rama, it's my smorgasbord. It's terrible.

My comfort foods are bread and butter, scrambled eggs, mashed potatoes and gravy, and macaroni and cheese. Scrambled eggs I can make in about two seconds, so it's instant gratification.

Now I buy sugar-free Jell-O. My husband and I buy Jell-O by the case at Costco, and I just pop the top. I put a little whipped cream on it, and it feels like dessert.

Ellen Alcala, sales and marketing account manager

Whatever Happened to "I'd Love to, but I'm Washing My Hair That Night"?

I've lost 160 pounds. At one point I was not able to stop emotional eating, so I went on a medically supervised liquid fast. After five months I started adding foods like chicken, fish, and vegetables. I've been on this for thirteen months now and am just about done with my weight loss.

In many ways weight was a protective thing for me. Sometimes the bigger and more unattractive we are, the less attention we get from men. But I finally came to my senses. My four-year-old daughter really influenced my decision to lose weight. I was at an unhealthy size and knew I needed to do something drastic so I could live a long life and be there for her.

After this long haul, I finally feel centered and have dealt with issues in my life regarding men and food. If you want to avoid relationships with men for a season, use something other than food, because all the attached issues are *so* not worth it. You also get medical problems, short life span, self-esteem issues, feelings of failure, and disrespectful treatment from the general public. Sabotaging yourself with food is the worst way to bow out of the game. Choose other options.

Michelle Willett, police dispatcher

Beef Up Your Attitude about Life

I could just eat chocolate and live. I love the texture in my mouth. My husband is Norwegian, and his parents will bring chocolate home from Norway that's very smooth. Our chocolate has a touch of bitterness to it and theirs doesn't.

Whenever I face crisis, I try to decide early on if I'm going to cope by overeating or not. I'm going to go one way or the other. When I'm stressed, I'm probably not really hungry but still want to grab food because it's an immediate source of pleasure. By recognizing at the beginning of a crisis that I'm not *actually* hungry, I try to break the habit of putting junk food in my mouth.

At the same time, I remind myself that if I don't eat well, I'm not going to be able to deal with a crisis in a logical way. If we don't at least get some kind of protein, our brains can't work well. I have a friend who works in the emergency room, and she told me when they have a patient who has attempted suicide, the first thing they do is feed them a steak because they are depressed and probably haven't been eating right. She said just getting the right food into their system can help them begin to think differently.

Renee Berge, technical writer

Need a Break from Life's Frantic Pace? Meet Me at Karen's for M&M's

I think chocolate is a common denominator for women. I've been at Karen's house on many occasions when there's been a big bowl of M&M's on the table!

Ideally I'd love to limit my chocolate to three or four times a week. Sometimes it's nice to have a little chocolate to finish off a meal. And of course, I crave chocolate around my period. One of my favorite more "daily" chocolates are Junior Mints.

Sometimes I overdose on chocolate and sugar in general, and when this happens I usually need to go back to the basics. For me that means making sure my time with the Lord is there. Making sure I'm depending on him for comfort and not on those Junior Mints!

I also know it is important for me to find time alone. To just stop. I struggle with a frantic pace like so many women do. It's important to just step back and find that time to be alone.

Nancy Rottmeyer, tax preparer

Don't Just Sit There, Do Something

After my divorce I would wake up in the middle of the night and drive through fast food places a couple of nights a week. I could really pile it on.

Although I didn't realize it at the time, the emotional component of my eating was that I was depressed over the divorce and had no idea what to do with the guilt and the changes. Eventually I had to deal with the guilt of disappointing my family with my marriage. I also joined Jenny Craig Diet Center and learned to eat better and not skip meals.

My advice? First, have peace with God. It's so important to seek him first.

Next, get yourself in groups and activities and stay busy with activities that are healthy. You can do all the praying you want, but if you don't take action and make lifestyle changes, you won't see change. Some people think all your struggles go away the minute you ask God to be Lord of your life. But there's still work to be done. When you have patterns or deep hurts, there may be actions you need to take like getting counseling or joining an eating program where they can teach you how to eat well and healthy again.

Terri Walters, dental hygienist and mother of two

Don't Diet—Energize

I used to have an eating disorder, and I think having gone through that makes a difference. My body is a temple. I want to be a good steward of my body just like with my money. That's where I try to stay mentally.

Women are obsessed with dieting, but I try to focus on being healthy and energetic. I've learned not to get on the scale all that often. I just watch my weight based on how my clothes are fitting. I don't get in the diet mode. Energy is really important, and that's what I try to focus on. If I eat this simple carb, I know I'm going to crash, so what can I eat that will make me feel better forty-five minutes from now?

Barb Rickford, full-time mother

The Dessert You Love to Hate

For dessert, chocolate is the only choice—everything else, no matter how elaborate, is just a disappointing substitute.

Recently my husband brought home a five-pound bag of M&M's, thinking I would be thrilled at the sight of them. Instead I found myself filled with dread over their intrusion into my normally safe, chocolate-free home. How is it that the thing you crave most can simultaneously inflict such a deep fear of losing self-control and gaining weight?

Diana Bender, printing specialist

Lord, It Was the Sister You Gave Me …

My predilection for dark chocolate came from my sister climbing into a high cupboard and sneaking into the baking chocolate when we were little kids and feeding it to me while I was sitting in my high chair.

Today I'd much rather eat just barely sweet dark chocolate than milk or white chocolate *any day*. And boy, am I thrilled to know that they are now saying chocolate is good for you.

Barbara Faust, job seeker

Weight Training?

My secret stash of chocolate is in the form of Ghirardelli 60 percent cocoa chocolate chips. It's amazing how fast a few at a time, ten times a day, can make a whole bag disappear when I'm in need of a little chocolate. It's just a tiny little chip. *Right!*

Eileen Somers, fitness club owner

Thinking Ahead

I used to struggle more with emotional eating. Now I'm getting better at identifying the real reason I'm eating. Usually it's a combination of low blood sugar and not meeting my emotional needs. I would eat more than I needed or eat when I wasn't even hungry.

Now that I'm a diabetic, food is a project for me—I have to plan to eat on a schedule and keep to it. I can't go too high or too low with my blood sugars. I drink a minimum of eight glasses of water and fit in a workout every day, even if it's a short time.

If I eat outside that schedule, I will eventually ask myself, "What's up? Why am I eating?" It's always an interesting conversation. If I'm anxious about something, I find myself looking for sugar, mostly in chocolate. Dark chocolate in particular tends to halt my "hunt" for chocolate. Then I get to face why I'm "hunting" in the first place, which turns into another interesting conversation between God and me.

Charlene Bruno, administrative assistant aka gofer

Now, for a Little Parting Gift ...

I can't keep any tempting snack foods in the house because I can't stop eating them. I've talked to a number of other people, and we all have this idea that we have to keep eating the snack foods in our house until they are gone. Now I won't keep snacks in the house unless I'm having company. I'm getting better about just tossing leftover snacks after the party. Often I'll just send the snacks home with someone else.

Laura Lisle, editor/writer

Desperately Seeking ... Something

I use food as a filler. If I'm bored, I eat. If I'm happy, I eat. If I'm sad, I eat.

Most of the time I give in to my chocolate cravings, but one thing my head knows—and most of the time my heart knows—is that I'm searching for something and I need to turn to God so he can fill whatever I truly need. I believe that when I'm eating even though my body doesn't physically need anything, it's often because something is off in my relationship with the Lord.

If I only ate when my body signaled that it needed food, I wouldn't have to worry as much about whether I'm working out enough or what I'm putting in my mouth. I believe God designed our bodies to tell us what we need, when we need it, and when we're satisfied. If we listened to those signals and counted on him for everything else, I believe, we wouldn't have such a need to fill up that void inside.

Shelly Johnson, business analyst

This *Is* the Mellow Kelly

I'm the only one in my immediate family who likes chocolate. I don't know what's wrong with my husband and son.

Chocolate keeps you in a good mood and keeps your attitude milder. Before I had my hysterectomy, I especially had to have chocolate. It helped make me a nicer person. When I'm sad, upset, tired, angry, or even happy—most anytime—I can find myself wanting to eat chocolate.

Chocolate mellows me out. At work I tell people they can bribe me with chocolate, but only one guy has tried it. He brought me some year-old stuff that looked pretty bad, so I told him he'd have to go stand in the corner.

Kelly Roberds, bank employee trainer

Chocolate: Medicine for a Broken Heart

Like a lot of my friends, I find that the pressures of grades and boyfriend problems can lead us to eat emotionally. If one of my friends breaks up with a guy, we all eat chocolate. When I broke up with my boyfriend last year, a friend gave me flowers and a box of Russell Stover chocolates.

I'm not tempted to snack much because my roommates and I don't keep much in our refrigerator. But if I'm having a stressful week, I'll go out and buy whatever I'm craving at that time. Sometimes if my roommates and I have cravings, we'll go swipe our meal card at the cafeteria just for ice cream. It's not very economical because each "meal" costs seven dollars, but sometimes you just want something sweet and you want an easy way to get it.

We can all turn to something like chocolate or whatever thinking it will help us get through life. There are a lot of girls on campus who will drink every weekend thinking it will help their problems, but it really doesn't.

Stephanie Leuders, college student

Mad about Chocolate

I binge when I feel frustrated or trapped, when I don't see an end to things, and when I don't see any options. I also binge when I'm angry. I want to *chomp* chocolate with almonds or *crunch* peanut M&M's. It used to be that when I felt angry, I could go running or do other activities, but it's harder now because I'm working and taking care of kids. I don't feel like I have time for other outlets to deal with my emotions.

It helps to identify my emotions and figure out better ways to deal with them, but I don't think most of us know how to do this. I can determine why I am angry, but I'm not always sure of better ways to deal with the anger.

So how *do* you deal with the anger? There are only so many physical things you can do. I go to a bag boxing class and I feel like I'm ripping the bag apart. I can punch the bag until I'm blue in the face and it's a great release. But how often can you do that? I only take the class once a week.

Chocolate is my favorite binge food. The other thing that I crave—and I try to have this before I get too angry—is a Starbucks white chocolate mocha. I call this my comfort food. I usually treat myself once a week. It

167

gives me something to look forward to. These days I'm doing better at controlling how much I eat.

Claire West, teacher

Too Much of a Good Thing

I was definitely a chocoholic even as a child. Whenever I would go to other people's homes, I would eat much more than my share of chocolate desserts. At Christmas parties I would sneak fudge and go off and eat it alone. In school I'd eat Nestlé Nesquik by the spoonful.

Apparently I ate *all* my lifetime chocolate allotment before the age of thirty, because now I'm deathly allergic to chocolate. It is a heavy cross to bear. Many people feel sorry for me, and I likewise feel sorry for myself.

I used to sample tiny bits of chocolate and end up sick in bed, sometimes for weeks. Now I dream about chocolate. I dream I'm at a banquet and eat these great chocolate desserts. I'll also eat chocolate chip cookies in my dreams, and they really do taste like chocolate.

Joli Storm, stay-at-home mom

Hey, Introduce Me to Your Friend, Will You?

I wouldn't say chocolate is my refuge because I enjoy chocolate all the time. Chocolate is my friend.

Not long after my husband and I married, we bought a five-pound package of chocolate chips. We never did make cookies because those chips were gone in a couple of weeks.

Lisa Dorman, stay-at-home mom

So, How Does That Make You Feel?

I love all the Dove dark chocolates, although Lindt I would not turn away.

Here are a couple of interesting things my midwife just told me. If you're nursing and your baby is constipated, eating chocolate will help. Also, apparently research now says that if a new mother eats chocolates, she is happier.

I noticed that right after my baby was born I was eating more chocolate. When he was a couple weeks old I was having five pieces of chocolate a day, and then I had less and less over time. At the time, my cravings definitely felt more physiological than psychological. Maybe it was chocolate's mood-enhancement qualities that helped me because I was just so tired and overwhelmed. As a new mom you just have that huge hormonal flux.

When I'm craving chocolate I don't really give much insightful thought as to why, even though I am a psychologist. I'll find chocolate chips in the cupboard that I would normally use for baking and eat those because, well, sometimes you just have to have any kind of chocolate you can find.

Julie Cox, psychologist

A Girl's Gotta Have Options

I think you have to look within yourself to handle your emotions and your cravings. Sometimes when I'm craving chocolate or some other comfort food, I make the choice not to eat it. I tell myself, "I don't need to do this to my body. I need to walk away and figure out another way to handle my emotions." Those times are rare, but I do have them. Sometimes instead of going for the chocolate, I make the choice to go for a walk, watch TV, read emails. I try to keep busy.

Donna Perot, special education paraeducator

The Bad News and Good News about Menopause

Eating struggles go out the window at menopause. Now you've got *big-time* food issues. You crave so many things. Things you used to eat, now you simply smell and gain five pounds. I swear you need to weigh yourself twice a day. Two pounds are easier to get off than twenty. You also need vitamins and supplements to help your mind when the estrogen drops. It's a mess. But it doesn't have to be if you're prepared.

Don't depend on your gynecologist to tell you anything. Do your own research. The book *Menopause for Dummies* is actually not just for menopause but for women dealing with hormones at all stages of life. Get knowledgeable. Talk to other women. Dr. Phil's wife started preparing for menopause in her thirties and believes that's the reason she didn't have a lot of struggles during that time. Whatever your age, it's not too soon to start.

Linda Hansen, Premier Design jewelry consultant

Escaping into Healthy Addiction

I want to escape from whatever I can't fix—or I *think* I can't fix.

When we're upset, it's easy to become addicted to whatever promises us the escape we crave. Whether we turn to work or alcohol or sleeping pills or junk food, it's all escape. I try to make a conscious choice in the beginning that I'm going to be "addicted" to something that's going to leave me with benefits by the time I'm over this crisis.

Exercise has been a lifesaver for me. If I can catch myself before falling into crisis, I force myself into an exercise routine. Normally when we get depressed we don't want to exercise. If I wait too long, I won't be able to get myself off the couch. But if I can catch it at the beginning, I'll start vigorously exercising. I've always been a runner, but I really throw myself into it. It's more than the fact that the endorphins help me understand things better. It's something I can become addicted to that's better for me than drinking alcohol or eating too much.

Renee Berge, technical writer

Real Life, Good Questions

Now that I have a toddler in the house, I have a lot more pretzels and Goldfish crackers around the house. I struggle now more than ever. But instead of thinking, "Oh my gosh, I've gained another ten pounds!" I try to get back to, "Okay, what's chaotic in my life? Bottom line, I have a two-year-old and I need to exercise more and be more active."

There are so many mixed messages out there—even in the church—to be thin. So much obsession with plastic surgery and body sculpting. I would do it, too. I know that sounds so shallow, but gosh, I work out and I eat pretty healthy, so part of me thinks "Why not?" Another part of me thinks, "This is not of the Lord; it's an obsession with self."

I think part of all this is a spiritual journey as well. Sometimes we have to ask ourselves, "What am I hiding? What am I not dealing with? What am I suppressing with food?" Sometimes if you deal with these issues, the food issues go away.

Barb Rickford, full-time mother

Mouth-Watering Memories

Recently I was overwhelmed with work and totally stressed. I went to the store to get cat food and they had Hamburger Helper on sale, and just the idea of it made me feel better. We used to eat this a lot growing up. I realized this wasn't an issue of being out of control but rather of getting comfort by being reminded of a great memory from home. There are certain things that to me symbolize good experiences from the past, like Dad making hamburgers from freshly ground beef and the taste of homemade malts.

Laura Lisle, editor/writer

You're Not the Boss of Me

I'm a mom and I have to give up a lot of what I want, so I'm going to eat whatever I feel like eating. I sacrifice a lot for my kids, so when I find something to eat, by golly, I'm going to eat whatever I want.

Maybe I crave freedom to do what I want to do. My husband may say, "No, you shouldn't eat that," and I think, "So what?" There's an underlying sense that I want some freedom, I want some space. I don't want anybody to tell me what to eat or what not to eat. I have a slight rebellion against my husband and kids because at times they are extremely demanding. Sometimes my eating is a rebellion against the demands of motherhood.

I've actually been praying about my eating habits because basically, if I want something, I eat it. I should be as big as a house, but I'm a normal weight. Sometimes I will chew gum or go exercise instead of snacking. Overall I do try to use healthy ingredients in my cooking and baking. Instead of sugar I use organic, unrefined evaporated cane juice, and I use unbleached flour. I'm still getting my sweets, but I'm just finding alternative ways to remain healthy.

Joli Storm, stay-at-home mom

Karen Scalf Linamen is a mother of two and the author or coauthor of numerous books, including the bestselling *Just Hand Over the Chocolate and No One Will Get Hurt*. Two of her books have received recognition as finalists for the ECPA Gold Medallion Award. She is also a frequent speaker at churches, women's retreats, and writers' conferences.

To invite Karen to speak at your next event, write to her at Karen@Karenlinamen.com.

More sanity-saving **humor,**
encouragement, and **advice** from
bestselling author Karen Scalf Linamen!